The Alphabet

Name _____

____✏️ a line to connect the dots. Follow the letters of the alphabet.

Start here.

D1404172

Missing Letters

 the missing letters.

a b ___ d e	f g h ___ j
k ___ m n o	___ q r s t
u v w x ___ z	
A ___ C D E	F G ___ I J
K L M N ___	P Q R ___ T
___ V W X Y Z	

What Comes First?

The first letter of each word is used to put words in alphabetical (ABC) order.

Example: <u>a</u>pple, <u>b</u>ee, <u>c</u>ar

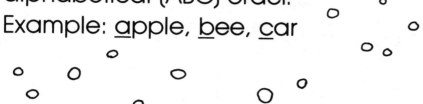

 the first letter of each word.

 the words in alphabetical order.

frog	jar	leaf
baby	dog	shoe
_____	_____	_____
1. _____	1. _____	1. _____
2. _____	2. _____	2. _____
wagon 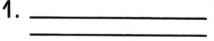	girl	nest 
ring	key	hen
_____	_____	_____
1. _____	1. _____	1. _____
2. _____	2. _____	2. _____

ABC Word Trail

Name _____

Take a trip through the zoo in alphabetical (ABC) order.

4

ABC Garden

Mr. Murphy wanted to plant his garden in ABC order.
Read the names of the vegetables in the word box.
Put the vegetables in the correct rows.

corn	tomatoes	lettuce	asparagus	potatoes
onions	beets	radishes	yams	spinach

1. asparagus
2. _____
3. _____
4. _____
5. _____
6. _____
7. _____
8. _____
9. _____
10. _____

ABC Order

Put the words in each box in ABC order.
~~✎~~ the numbers 1, 2, 3 on the lines.

 doll   _2_

 game   _3_

 block   _1_

 apple   ____

 cookie   ____

 milk   ____

 hat   ____

 coat   ____

 mitten   ____

 car   ____

 truck   ____

 jeep   ____

 monkey ____

 turtle   ____

 cow   ____

 pencil   ____

 desk   ____

 book   ____

Compound Words

Sometimes two words are put together to make one new word. The new word is called a **compound** word. Example: cow + boy = cowboy

Look at the pictures below. Add the words together and  a new word on the line.

rain + coat = _____

door + bell = _____

dog + house = _____

up + stairs = _____

pan + cake = _____

horse + shoe = _____

Two Words in One

Name ____________________

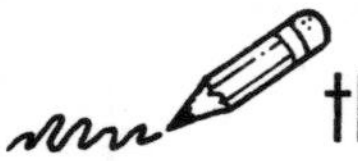 the two words that make up each compound word below.

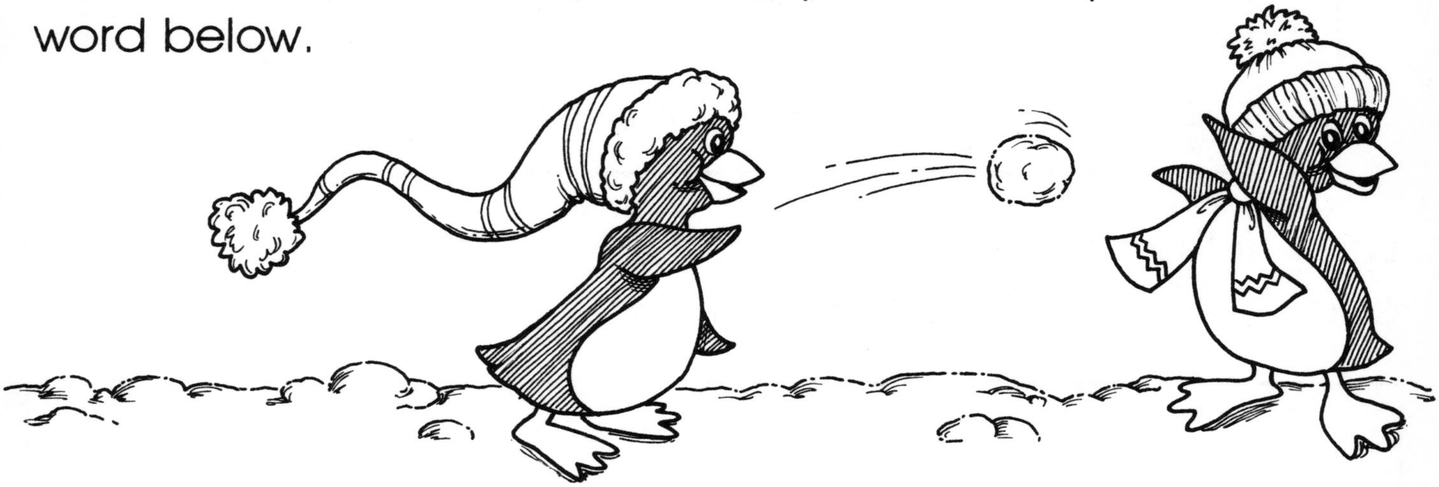

snowball 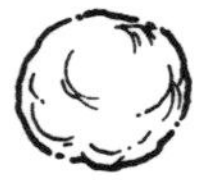

raincoat 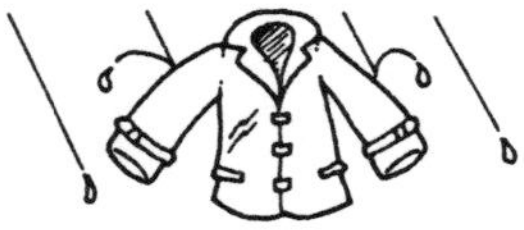

airplane 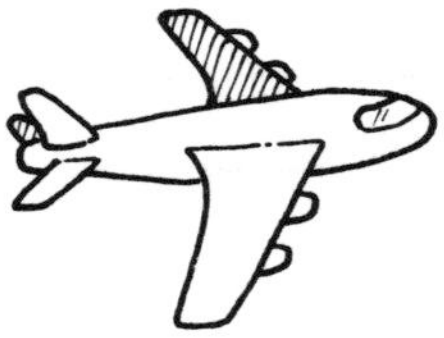

watermelon 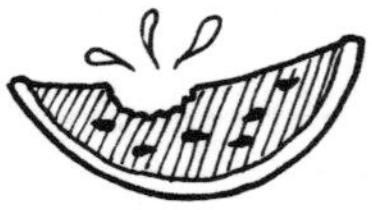

haircut 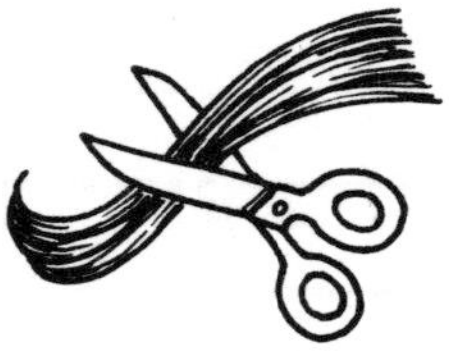

football 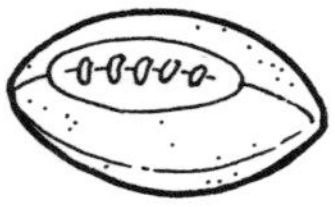

fingernail 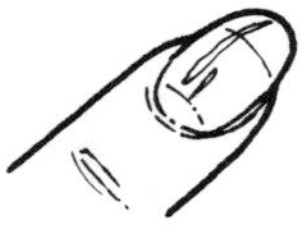

sunshine 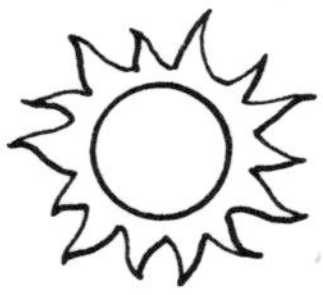

Writing
Compound Words

Read each sentence. ___✏ a line under the two
words in each sentence that can make a new word.
〰✏ the compound word on the line.

_____

1. A bird that is black is a _____ .

2. A horse that can race is a _____ .

_____

3. A cloth that covers the table is a _____ .

4. A room where you have a bed is a _____ .

_____

5. A book with a story is a _____ .

_____

6. A bowl used to hold fish is a _____ .

Sound Words

Some words tell about sounds and about actions that go with sounds. Example: lightning - crash
owl - hoot

Find a word from the word bank that describes each picture.  the word under the picture.

Word Bank		
chirp	pop	crash
bang	boom	gulp

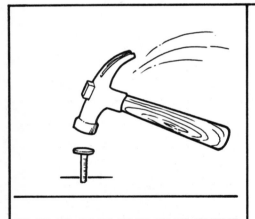

_____
- - - - - - - - -

_____
- - - - - - - - -

_____
- - - - - - - - -

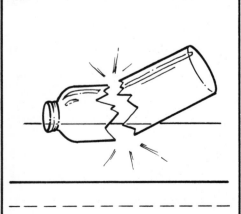

_____
- - - - - - - - -

_____
- - - - - - - - -

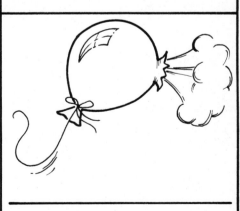

_____
- - - - - - - - -

Sound Riddles

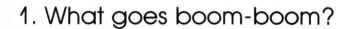a line from each riddle to the right picture.

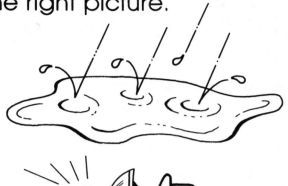

1. What goes boom-boom?

2. What goes splish-splash?

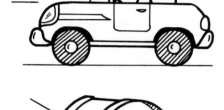

3. What goes honk-honk?

4. What goes tick-tock?

5. What goes buzz-buzz?

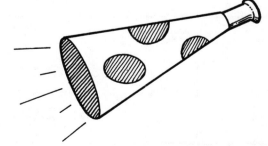

6. What goes toot-toot?

Finding Opposites

Read each sentence. ✏ the word that means the opposite of the underlined word.

1. The  is <u>on</u>.	off	hard	wet
2. The  is bright at <u>night</u>.	big	hot	day
3. The  is <u>sad</u>.	go	happy	top
4. The  is <u>high</u>.	low	soft	cold
5. Those  look <u>old</u>.	over	new	up
6. The is <u>open</u>.	tall	short	closed

12

Opposites

Below each word, ✎ a word that means the opposite. Use the word bank to help you.

Word Bank			
lost	down	go	low
left	sad	empty	dry

won

stop

full

happy

_ _ _ _ _ _ _

wet

high

right

up

13

Matching Opposites

Name _____

a line to match opposites.

old

front

laugh

fat

big

day

back

cry

new

thin

night

little

Almost Alike

Some words have the same or almost the same meaning.
Example: She is glad.
          She is happy.

Read the words. ✏️ the word that means almost the same as the first word.

1. big	cold loud large
2. yell	shout eat jump
3. small	good thin little
4. smile	tall grin soft
5. boat	talk ship hop
6. look	see fall laugh

Almost Alike

Read the sentences. Find a word in the word bank that means almost the same as the circled word. it on the line.

Word Bank				
shut	big	start	sleepy	talk

1. The storybook is (large). _____

2. The baby grew very (tired). _____

3. The race should (begin) soon. _____

4. (Speak) into the microphone. _____

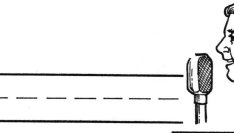

5. The door is (closed). _____

Almost the Same Meaning

Read the words in the word box.  two words
under each picture.

rock	start	road	begin	street	stone
shut	sad	talk	unhappy	speak	closed

Same or Opposite?

🖍 yellow the spaces that have word pairs with opposite meanings.

🖍 blue the spaces that have word pairs with the same meanings.

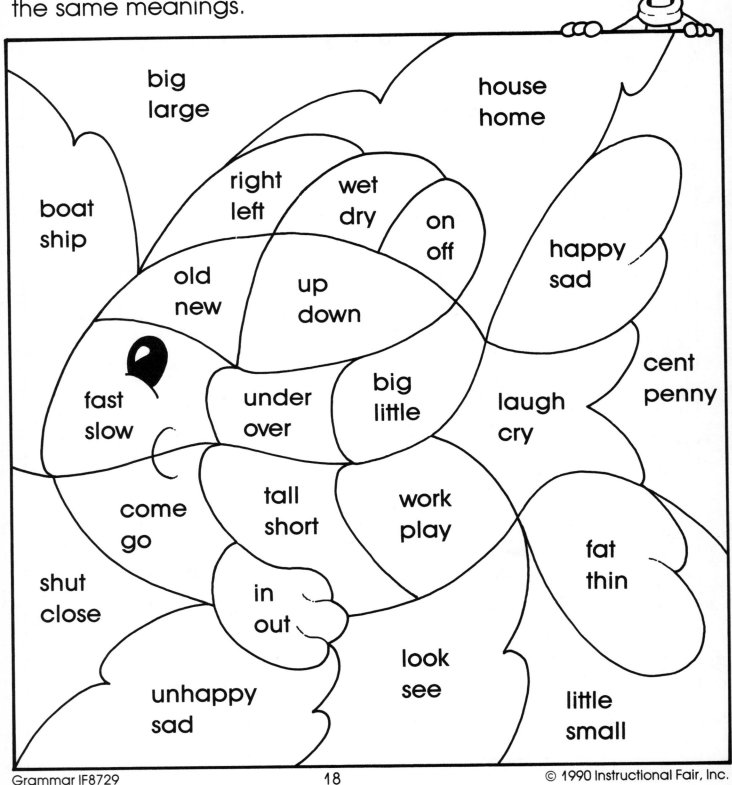

big
large

house
home

boat
ship

right
left

wet
dry

on
off

happy
sad

old
new

up
down

fast
slow

under
over

big
little

laugh
cry

cent
penny

come
go

tall
short

work
play

fat
thin

shut
close

in
out

look
see

little
small

unhappy
sad

Words That Sound Alike

Words that sound the same may not mean the same or be spelled the same.
Example: I know how to read.
             I have no pencil.

Read the sentences below. ✐ the correct word on each line.

1. Jim _____ the cookies.

ate
eight

2. Sally has _____ pencils.

to
two

3. The _____ is bumpy.

rode
road

4. _____ can ride a bike.

eye
I

5. Can you _____ the picture?

see
sea

6. Tom _____ up the balloon.

blew
blue

Words That Sound the Same

Some words **sound** the same but do not have the
same meanings or spellings.
Example: I **know** how to spell.
          I have **no** book.

a word that sounds like each of these but is
spelled in a different way. Use the word bank below
to help you.

1. blew _____   5. some _____

2. road _____   6. new _____

3. ate _____   7. right _____

4. two _____   8. not _____

Word Bank

blue	too	knot	write
sum	rode	eight	knew

Do They Sound Alike?

Name _____

only the balloons with words that sound alike.

frog
fox

I
eye

eye
ear

pie
pig

right
write

sun
son

no
know

so
sew

bat
box

one
won

Sound Alike Words

the correct word to finish each sentence.

1. Billy went swimming in the (sea, see).
2. The (sun, son) was shining.
3. He saw a boat with a large (sale, sail).
4. Billy and Cindy put sand in a (pail, pale).
5. They (wood, would) like to visit the seashore again.

Grammar IF8729

22

Sentences

Name _____

 the first word of each sentence. Remember to begin with a capital letter.

1. _____ class went to the airport.
   (our)

2. _____ jets were noisy.
   (big)

3. _____ helicopter landed.
   (one)

4. _____ saw some men washing airplanes.
   (we)

5. _____ pilot wore a uniform.
   (the)

Sentence Parts —
The Naming Part

A sentence has two parts — the naming part and the action part. The **naming part** tells **whom** or **what** the sentence is about.
Example: **The chimp** rode a bike.

____ a line under the naming part in each sentence below.

1. Our class had a picnic in the park.

2. Some teachers played ball with us.

3. The hot dogs were good to eat.

4. Big trees grew along the road.

5. A man was jogging.

6. A woman was fishing in the lake.

Writing the Naming Part

Read the naming parts in the tent.
✏️ one of the naming parts to begin each sentence.

Rain
Black clouds
A big wind
The campfire
Todd and Clint
The old green tent

1. _____ went camping.

2. _____ was hard to set up.

3. _____ blew the trees.

4. _____ filled the sky.

5. _____ ran off the tent.

6. _____ went out.

Sentence Parts —
The Action Part

> The **action part** of a sentence tells what the naming part is **doing** or **did**.
> Example: Bill **throws the ball**.

___a line under the action part in each sentence below.

1. My family walked to the zoo.

2. The seals swam in a pool of water.

3. A monkey climbed a tree.

4. Two big elephants swung their trunks.

5. A striped tiger paced in its cage.

6. The giraffe stretched its long neck.

Grammar IF8729   26   © 1990 Instructional Fair, Inc.

Writing the Action Part

Name _____

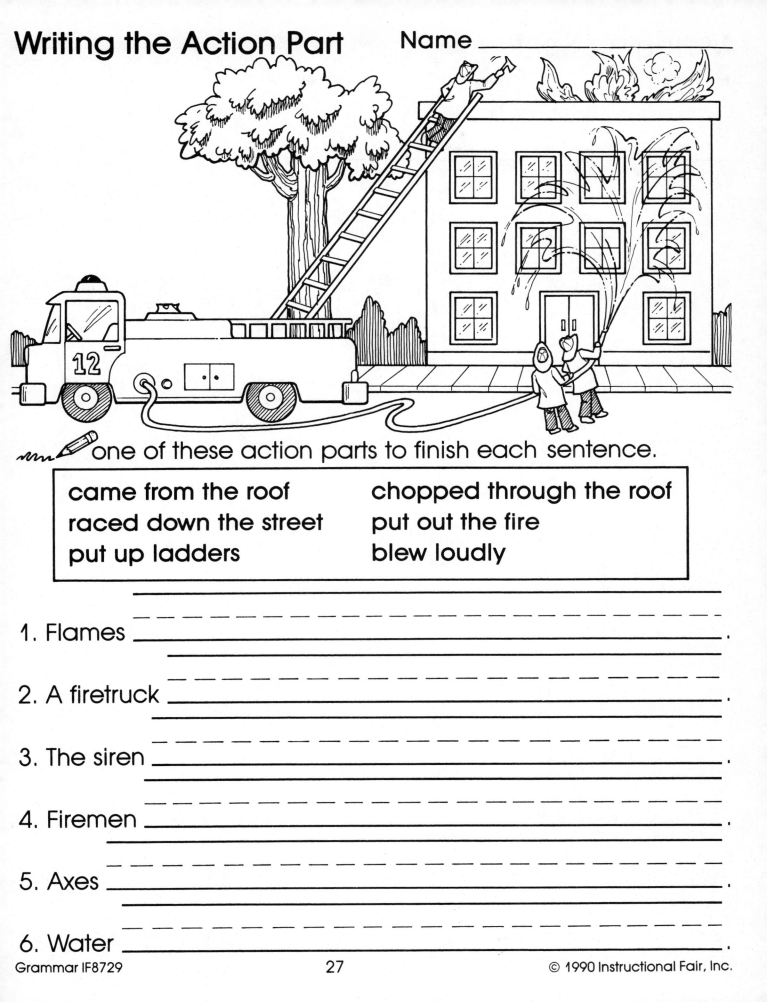

✏️ one of these action parts to finish each sentence.

came from the roof	chopped through the roof
raced down the street	put out the fire
put up ladders	blew loudly

1. Flames _____.

2. A firetruck _____.

3. The siren _____.

4. Firemen _____.

5. Axes _____.

6. Water _____.

Matching Sentence Parts

Name _____

Match a naming part with an action part.
Read the sentences you make.

A shiny bug •   • hopped away.

Two birds •   • sat on a rock.

A white rabbit •   • ran up a tree.

The green turtle •   • flew to a fence.

A small chipmunk •   • barked at the turtle.

My dog •   • closed his shell.

Telling Sentences

Some sentences tell something.
Telling sentences begin with a capital letter.
Telling sentences end with a period.
Example: The bird sings.

✏ only the sentences that tell.

1. Two turtles sat on a log.

2. One turtle fell off.

3. Did you see him?

4. He swam away.

5. The water is cold.

6. Can you swim?

A Statement

Some sentences tell something.
They are called statements.
A statement begins with a capital letter.
A statement ends with a period.
Example: [T]he teacher helped the child[.]

these statements correctly.

1. jenny planted a seed

_____

- - - - - - - - - - - - - - - - - - - -

_____

2. she gave it water

_____

- - - - - - - - - - - - - - - - - - - -

_____

3. it sat in the sunshine

_____

- - - - - - - - - - - - - - - - - - - -

_____

4. the plant began to grow

- - - - - - - - - - - - - - - - - - - -

_____

5. leaves grew large

_____

- - - - - - - - - - - - - - - - - - - -

_____

6. a flower opened

- - - - - - - - - - - - - - - - - - - -

_____

Writing a Telling Sentence

Name _____

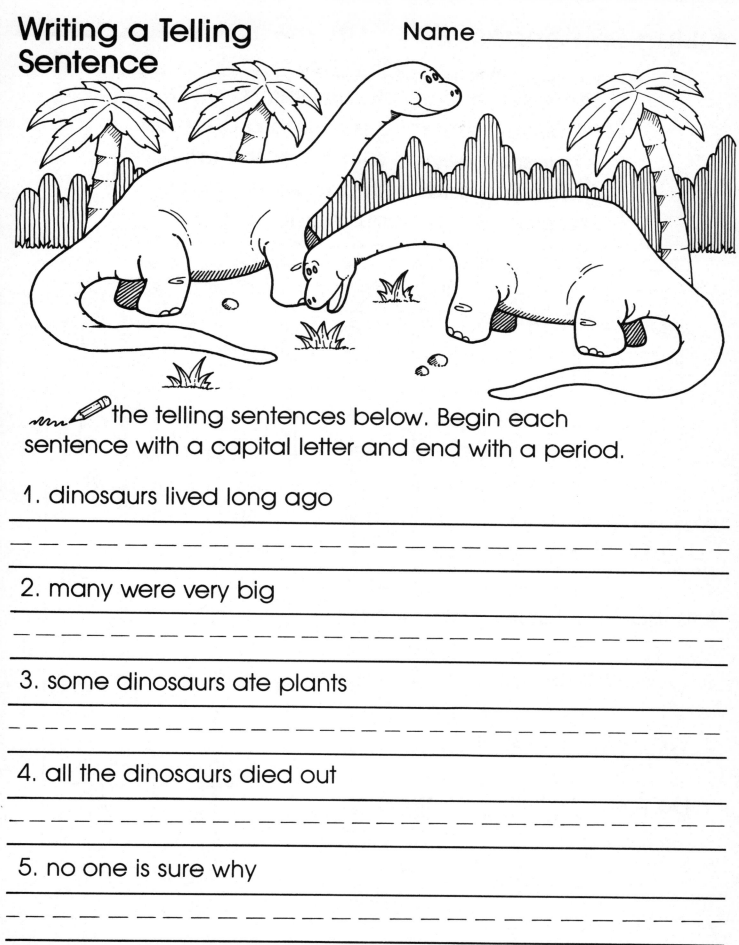

✏ the telling sentences below. Begin each sentence with a capital letter and end with a period.

1. dinosaurs lived long ago

_____

_____

2. many were very big

_____

_____

3. some dinosaurs ate plants

_____

_____

4. all the dinosaurs died out

_____

_____

5. no one is sure why

_____

_____

Asking Sentences

Some sentences ask something.
An asking sentence is called a question.
A question begins with a capital letter.
A question ends with a question mark.
Example: What is your name?

only the questions.

1. Is that your house?

2. There are two pictures on the wall.

3. Where do you sleep?

4. Do you watch TV in that room?

5. Which coat is yours?

6. The kitten is asleep.

A Question

> Some sentences ask something.
> An asking sentence is called a question.
> A question begins with a capital letter.
> A question ends with a question mark.
> Example: [H] ow tall are you [?]

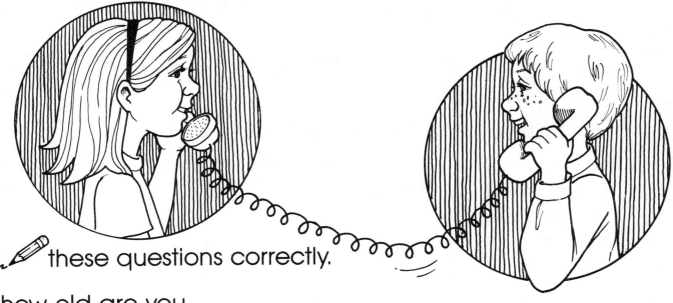

these questions correctly.

1. how old are you

_____

_____

2. are you in second grade

_____

_____

3. who is your teacher

_____

_____

4. did you read that book

_____

_____

5. where do you live

_____

_____

33

Writing a Question

Name _____

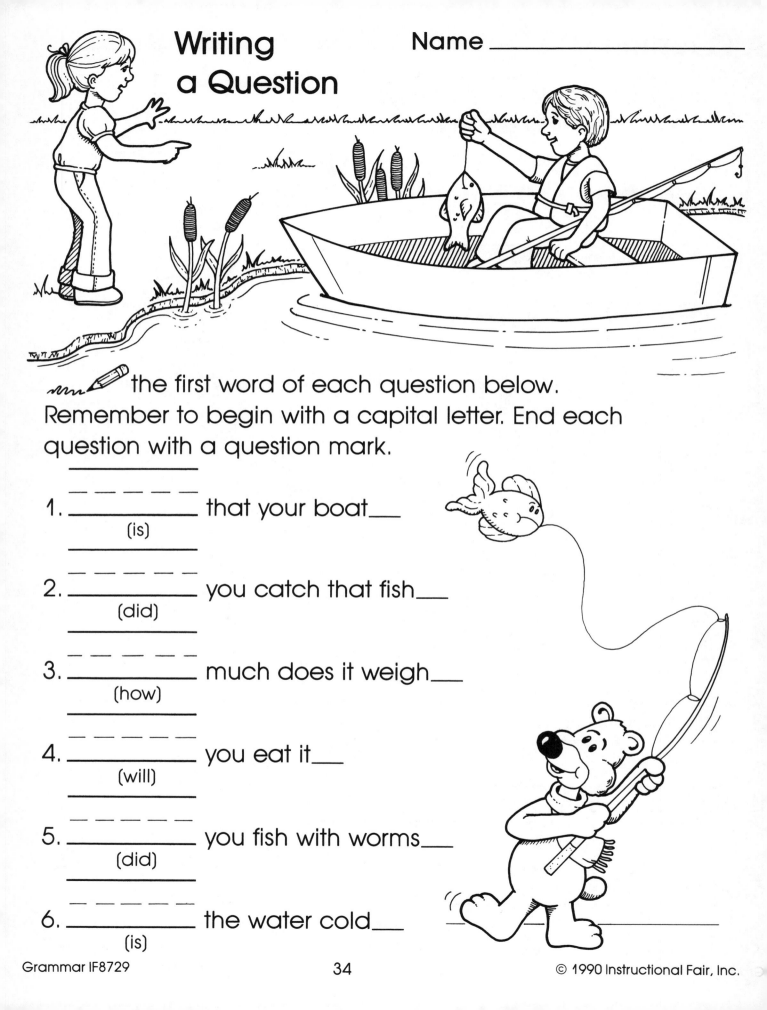

the first word of each question below. Remember to begin with a capital letter. End each question with a question mark.

1. _____ that your boat___
   (is)

2. _____ you catch that fish___
   (did)

3. _____ much does it weigh___
   (how)

4. _____ you eat it___
   (will)

5. _____ you fish with worms___
   (did)

6. _____ the water cold___
   (is)

Statement or Question?

Read these sentences.

✎ "S" next to each statement.

✎ "Q" next to each question.

1. Our school bus is yellow. _____

2. Do you ride the bus? _____

3. Chuck walks to school. _____

4. Last week our bus had a flat tire. _____

5. Does the bus stop in front of your house? _____

6. Did you ever miss the bus? _____

Period or Question Mark?

Name _____

Put a period or question mark in each box below.

1. Ryan and Emily had a picnic ☐

2. They fed bread to the ducks ☐

3. Do you think the ducks will fly away ☐

4. Will they come back next summer ☐

5. Ants crawled on the table ☐

6. Are they hungry, too ☐

Period or Question Mark?

Put a period or a question mark at the end of each sentence.

1. Can the fish jump out of the tank ☐

2. Two snakes are in that cage ☐

3. How much does that turtle cost ☐

4. Yes, I already have a dog ☐

5. His name is King ☐

6. Do you have a dog ☐

37

Sentence Sense

The words in a sentence must be in an order that makes sense.

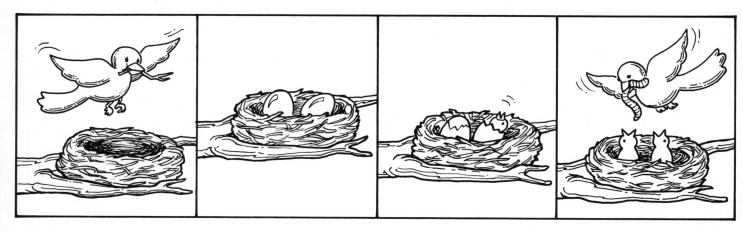

Put these words in the correct order. the sentences on the lines.

1. nest. bird The makes a

_____

_____

2. some lays eggs. She

_____

_____

3. are eggs The blue.

_____

_____

4. open. The crack eggs

_____

_____

5. The hungry. are birds baby

_____

_____

Scrambled Sentences

Name _____

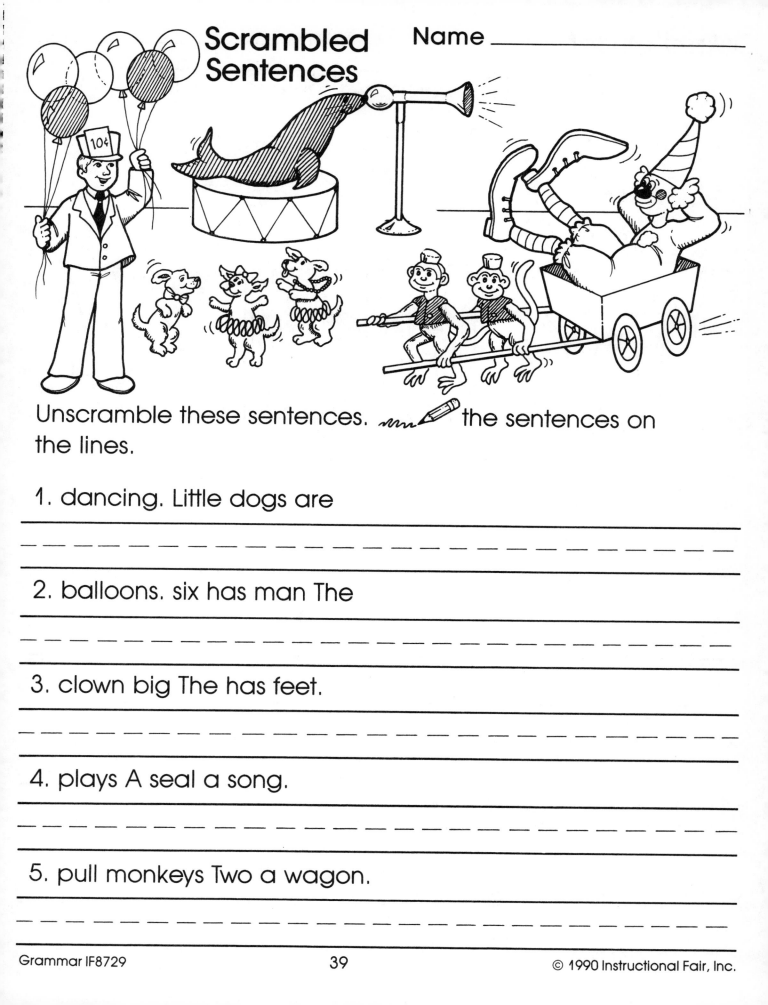

Unscramble these sentences. ✏️ the sentences on the lines.

1. dancing. Little dogs are

_____

_ _ _ _ _ _ _ _ _ _ _ _ _ _ _ _ _ _ _

2. balloons. six has man The

_____

_ _ _ _ _ _ _ _ _ _ _ _ _ _ _ _ _ _ _

3. clown big The has feet.

_____

_ _ _ _ _ _ _ _ _ _ _ _ _ _ _ _ _ _ _

4. plays A seal a song.

_____

_ _ _ _ _ _ _ _ _ _ _ _ _ _ _ _ _ _ _

5. pull monkeys Two a wagon.

_____

_ _ _ _ _ _ _ _ _ _ _ _ _ _ _ _ _ _ _

Word Order

> To make sense, words in a sentence must be in order.

Make a sentence by putting each group of words in the correct order.

1. watched a parade. We

_____

_ _

2. tricks. did clown A

_____

_ _

3. a horse. man A rode

_____

_ _

4. lions Big in cage. a were

_____

_ _

5. marched band by. A

_____

_ _

Word Order

Name _____

> Changing the order of the words in a sentence may change the meaning.
>
> Example: The dog chased the cat.
>   The cat chased the dog.

Read the sentence pairs.

✏ the sentence that goes with the picture.

The boy hit the ball. The ball hit the boy.	
The giant watched the elf. The elf watched the giant.	
The teacher read to the girl. The girl read to the teacher.	
The baby laughed at the father. The father laughed at the baby.	
The frog jumped over the rabbit. The rabbit jumped over the frog.	

Jellybean Jumble

Name _____

The words in each jar are mixed up. Put them in order to make sense. 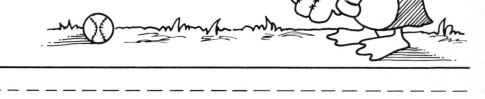 the sentences.

We ball played today.

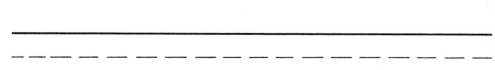

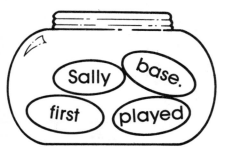
Sally base. first played

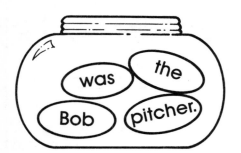
was the Bob pitcher.

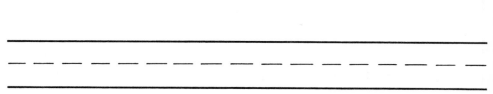

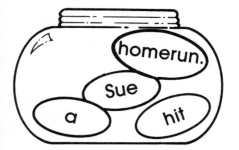
homerun. Sue a hit

won Our the game. team

Naming Words

A naming word names a person, place or thing.
Example: person—nurse, boy
         place —park, store
         thing —drum, tree

In the word box below, ✏ only the words that
name a person, place or thing.

teacher	zoo	dog	hat	library
runs	is	cowboy	the	up

Use the **naming words** you circled to label each
picture below.

_____   _____   _____

_____   _____   _____

43

Nouns

Name _____

A noun is a naming word.
A noun names a person, place or thing.
For example: person: nurse
                      place: town
                      thing: tree

Find **two** nouns in each sentence below.
 them.

1. The pig has a curly tail.	
2. The hen is sitting on her nest.	
3. A horse is in the barn.	
4. The goat has horns.	
5. The cow has a calf.	
6. The farmer is painting the fence.	

Words That Name Things

Read the naming words below. ✏️ the correct
naming word for each picture of a person, place
or thing.

barn	farmer	pig
boy	tree	horse
girl	ducks	sun

Person, Place or Thing

Name _____

✎ these naming words in the correct box.

girl	park	truck
vase	leaf	fireman
fish	doctor	zoo
school	store	ball
man	library	baby

Person

Place

Thing

More Naming

Name _____

_____ the correct naming word in each sentence.

ducks	dog	sun
boys	tree	bird

1. A big _____ grows in the park.

2. The _____ is in the sky.

3. A _____ digs a hole.

4. Three _____ swim in the water.

5. A _____ sits on her nest.

6. Two _____ fly a kite.

Person, Place or Thing

Name _____

✏ _____ the correct noun in each sentence.
Use the picture and the word bank to help you.

Word Bank		
apple	clock	hand
books	chalkboard	children

1. The _____ are in school.

2. A round _____ is on the wall.

3. Tim is writing on the _____.

4. One girl is raising her _____.

5. There are _____ on the shelves.

6. The teacher has an _____ on her desk.

Scrambled Nouns

Name _____

Unscramble the letters. ✎ the noun on the line.

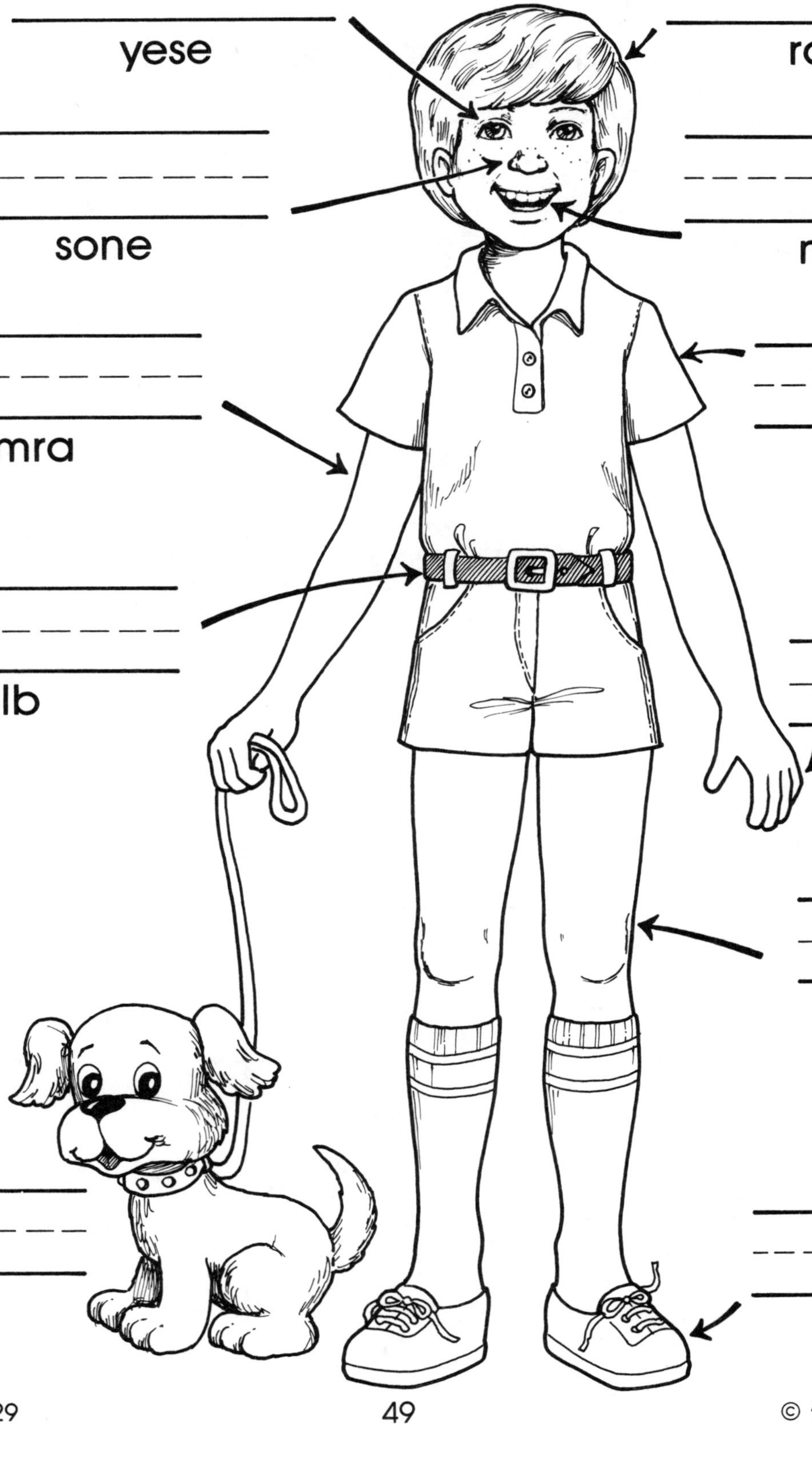

yese

raih

sone

mthou

smra

hrtis

telb

dahn

gel

dgo

oesh

© 1990 Instructional Fair, Inc.

Naming More Than One

Some words name one person, place or thing.
Example: balloon, girl, egg
Some words name more than one person, place or thing. We often add "s" to a word to make it show more than one.
Example: balloons, girls, eggs

Read the words. Draw a around the word that tells about the picture.

star stars	bike bikes	pencil pencils
fork forks	bug bugs	mitten mittens
bird birds	dog dogs	jeep jeeps

One or More Than One?

Name _____

✎ the correct word under each picture.

dish   dishes

car   cars

frog   frogs

hat   hats

glass   glasses

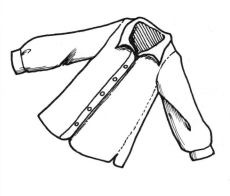

shirt   shirts

cloud   clouds

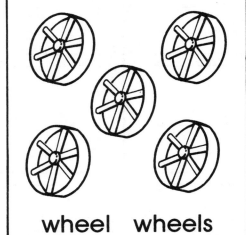

wheel   wheels

church   churches

One or More Than One?

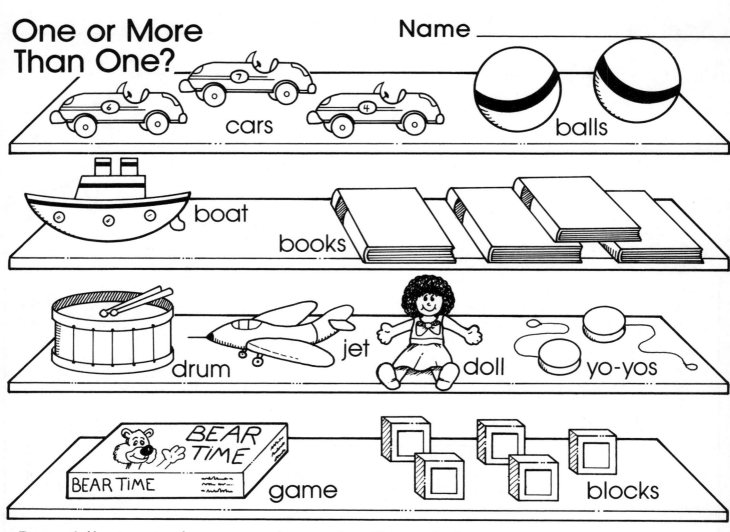

cars

balls

boat

books

drum

jet

doll

yo-yos

game

blocks

Read the naming words under the pictures.

each word under **One** or **More Than One**.

One	More Than One

Adding "s"

A plural word means more than one. We add "s" to most nouns to make a plural.
Example: Sid has **one dog**.
Jerry has **two dogs**.

✎ the plural form of the words below.

1. flower	_____	
2. girl	_____	
3. squirrel	_____	
4. toy	_____	
5. wagon	_____	
6. turtle	_____	

Adding "es"

Name _____

A plural word means more than one. We usually add "es" to words that end in **x**, **s**, **ss**, **sh** or **ch**.
Example: He filled **one box** with sand.
He filled **four boxes** with sand.

✎ the plural form of each word below.

1. peach _____

2. brush _____

3. fox _____

4. dress _____

5. bus _____

6. witch _____

Plural Review

Name _____

Decide if the words mean **one** or **more than one**.

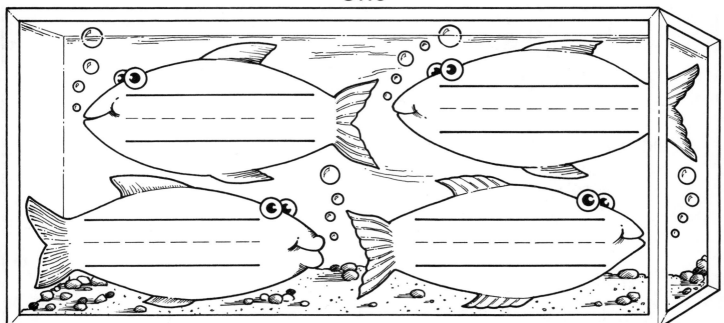 the words on the fish in the correct tank.

kites	star	chick	foxes
mitten	cats	matches	lunch

One

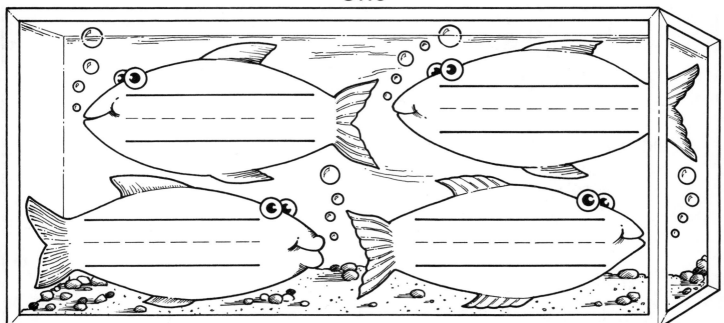

More Than One (Plural)

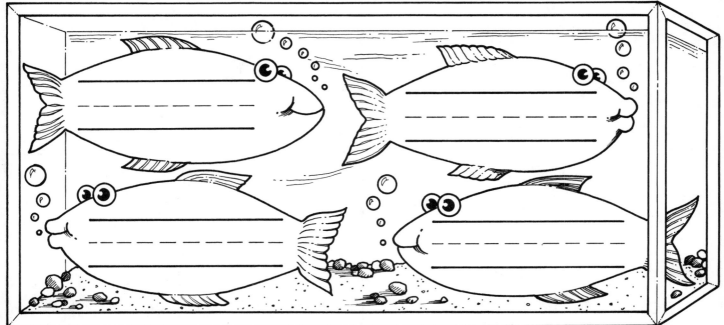

Adding " 's"

> Add " 's" to a noun to show who or what **owns** something.
> Example: The dog belongs to Larry.
>   It is Larry's dog.

✏ the correct word under each picture.

The _____ nose is big.
clown   clowns   clown's

This is _____ coat.
Bettys   Betty's   Betty

I know _____ brother.
Burt's   Burt   Burts

The _____ hat is pretty.
girls   girl   girl's

That is the _____ ball.
kitten's   kitten   kittens

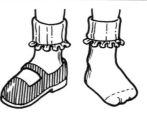

My _____ shoe is missing.
sisters   sister   sister's

The _____ coach is Mr. Hall.
teams   team's   team

The _____ cover is torn.
book's   books   book

Ownership

An " 's" at the end of a word shows ownership.

Read the sentence pairs. Finish the second sentence to show ownership. The first one has been done for you.

1. The red wagon belongs to Mike. It is ____Mike's____ red wagon.	
2. The fur of the rabbit is soft. The _____ fur is soft.	
3. The name of my friend is Donna. My _____ name is Donna.	
4. The tail of the pig is curly. The _____ tail is curly.	
5. The tire of the bike is flat. The _____ tire is flat.	
6. That mitten belongs to Jane. That is _____ mitten.	

Action Words

Name _____

An action word tells what a person or thing can do.

Example: Fred kicks the ball.

Read the action words below. ✏ the ones **you** can do.

jump 	skate 
swim 	sleep 
sing 	hop 
talk 	read 

Match the Action Word!

Name _____

Find the action word in each sentence. ✏ it.
✏ a line to match each sentence with the correct picture.

1. The dog barks.

2. The bird flies.

3. A fish swims.

4. One monkey swings.

5. A turtle crawls.

6. A boy talks.

Verbs

A verb is an action word. A verb tells what a person or thing does or did.
Example: Jane **reads** a book.

Find the verb in each sentence below and ✏ it.

1. The bear climbs a ladder.

2. Two tiny dogs dance.

3. A boy eats cotton candy.

4. A woman swings on a trapeze.

5. The clown falls down.

6. A tiger jumps through a ring.

What a Person or Thing Can Do

Name _____

Read the action words in the word box.
 the correct word under each picture.

eat	laugh	swing
build	sit	throw

Writing Verbs

Name _____

Word Bank

beat	sang	told
danced	sat	wore

✏️ _____ a verb in each sentence below. Use the word bank to help you.

1. The boys and girls _____ around the campfire.

2. They _____ songs.

3. Brian _____ a drum.

4. Jerry and Helen _____ Indian costumes.

5. They _____ around the campfire.

6. The teacher _____ stories.

More Action Words

Look at the pictures. Read the action words. Write an action word in each sentence below.

1. The boy _____ at the animals.

2. A snake _____ over a rock.

3. The puppy _____ .

4. Two rabbits _____ .

5. Many fish _____ in a tank.

6. A bird _____ .

63

Using "Is" and "Are"

Name _____

> Use "is" when talking about one person or thing.
> Use "are" when talking about more than one.
> Example: The girl is reading.
> The girls are reading.

✎ "is" or "are" in the sentences below.

1. The baby _____ sleeping.

2. Cookies _____ good to eat.

3. Apples _____ sweet and crisp.

4. A boy _____ painting a picture.

5. The ducks _____ in the pond.

6. The girl _____ riding her bike.

Using "Is," "Are" and "Am"

Use "is" and "are" to tell about now.
Use "is" to tell about one person or thing.
Use "are" to tell about more than one.
Use "are" with the word "you."
Use "am" with the word "I."

"is," "are" or "am" in each sentence below.

1. The lake _____ deep.

2. I _____ fishing.

3. Sally _____ baiting a hook.

4. Dan and Chuck _____ coming to our cabin.

5. We _____ going to cook the fish for dinner.

6. You _____ invited, too.

65

In the Past

A verb can tell about something that happened in the past. Some verbs add "ed" to tell about the past.

Example: Today, Tara and Jim **walk** to school.

Yesterday, Tara and Jim **walked** to school.

the correct verb in each sentence.

1. Last week, I _____ in the park.
   (play, played)

2. Yesterday, I _____ in the lake.
   (fish, fished)

3. Today, I will _____ Dad.
   (help, helped)

4. I _____ to help Dad.
   (like, liked)

5. My sisters _____ their room two hours ago.
   (clean, cleaned)

6. Now they _____ Dad, too.
   (help, helped)

Now or In the Past?

Name _____

 these verbs in the correct Time Machine.

play	pull	barked	jumped	danced
looked	laugh	walk	listen	lived

Now   In the Past

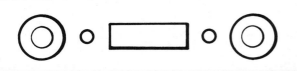

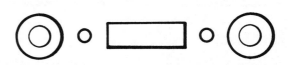

Using "Was" and "Were"

Name _____

Use "was" and "were" to tell about something that happened in the past.

Use "was" to tell about **one** person or thing.

Use "were" to tell about **more than one** person or thing.

Always use "were" with the word "you."

"was" or "were" in each sentence below.

1. Lois _____ in the second grade last year.

2. She _____ eight years old.

3. Carmen and Judy _____ friends.

4. They _____ on the same soccer team.

5. I _____ on the team, too.

6. You _____ too young to play.

Using "Give," "Gives" and "Gave"

Name _____

> Use "give" and "gives" to tell about now.
> Use "gave" to tell about the past.

✏ "give," "gives" or "gave" in each sentence below.

1. Trisha _____ a party last week.

2. Please _____ me the book.

3. I _____ my dog some water every day.

4. Jill _____ the jacket to me yesterday.

5. She _____ me a turn each day.

6. The teacher always _____ a test on Friday.

Using "See," "Sees" and "Saw"

Name _____

Use "see" or "sees" to tell about now.
Use "saw" to tell about the past.

Write "see," "sees" or "saw" in each sentence below.

1. I _____ the picture Tom is painting now.

2. He _____ the bird at the zoo last week.

3. Betsy _____ something out the window now.

4. She _____ a rainbow yesterday.

5. We _____ clouds in the sky today.

6. Last week, I _____ a cloud shaped like a pig.

Verb Review

Name _____

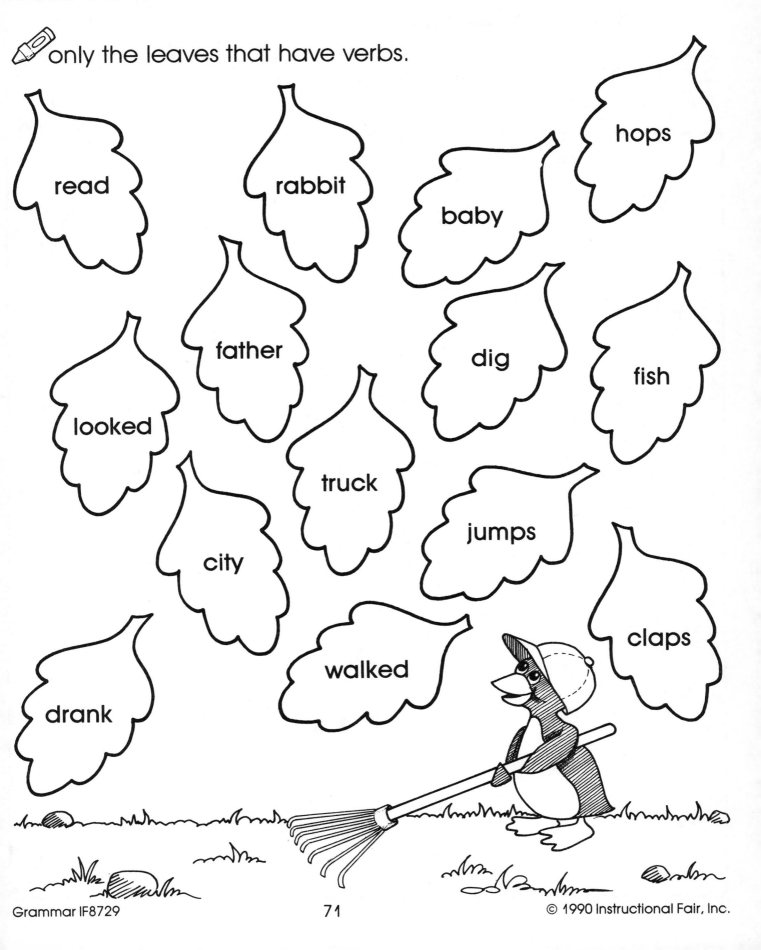

✏️ only the leaves that have verbs.

read

rabbit

hops

baby

father

dig

fish

looked

truck

jumps

city

claps

walked

drank

Review — Naming Words and Action Words

Name _____

✏️ the spaces with **naming** words ▸ green.
✏️ the spaces with **action** words ▸ pink.

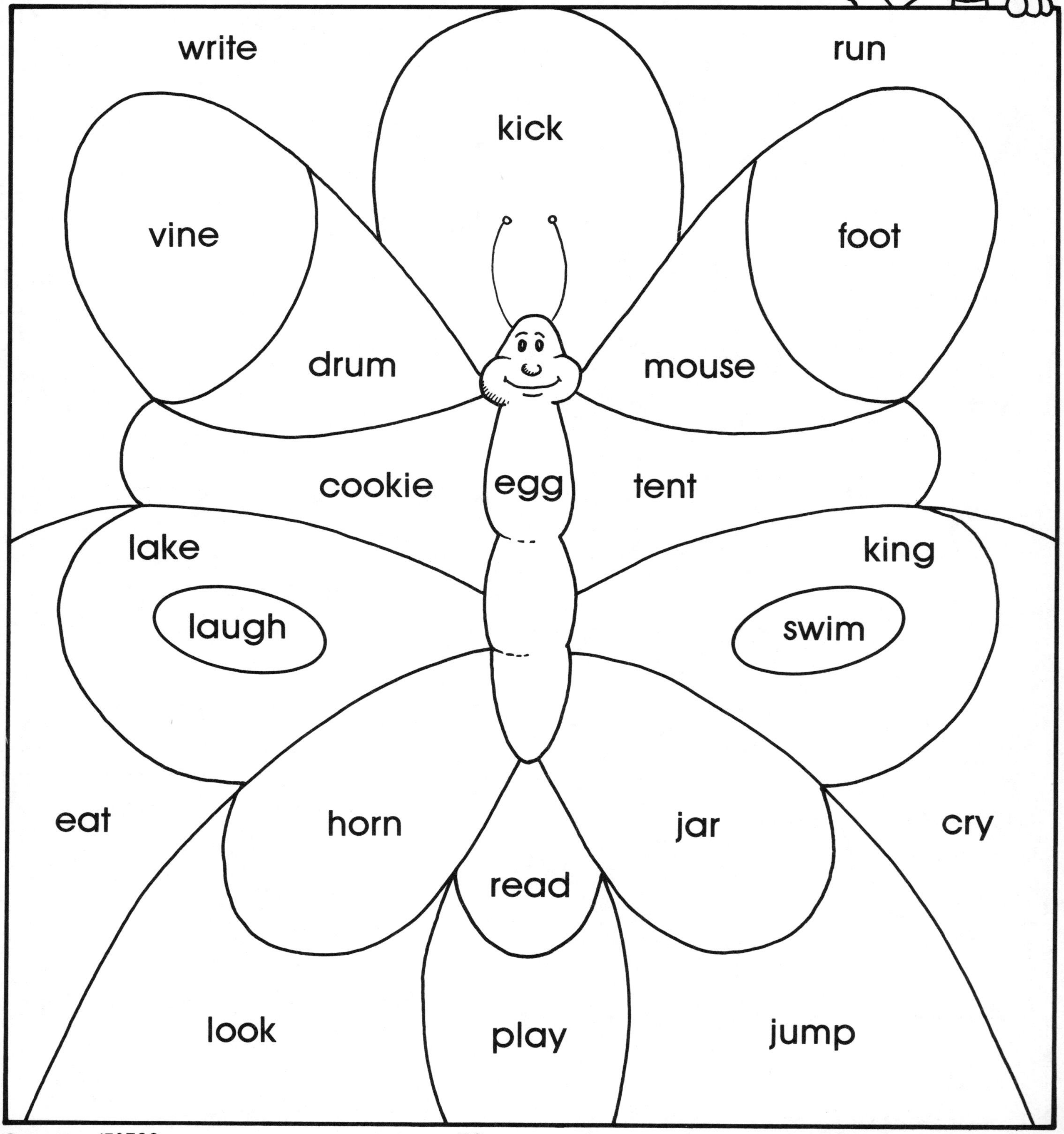

write

run

kick

vine

foot

drum

mouse

cookie   egg   tent

lake

king

laugh

swim

eat   horn   jar   cry

read

look   play   jump

Review — Nouns and Verbs

✎ one noun and one verb under each picture.
Use the word bank to help you.

Word Bank			
skate	leaves	fall	dog
flies	girls	jet	digs
sleeps	hop	baby	boys

noun   verb   noun   verb

noun   verb   noun   verb

noun   verb   noun   verb

In Place of a Noun

The words "he," "she," "it" and "they" can be used in place of a noun.

Example: **Jane** caught the ball.

She caught the ball.

Read the sentence pairs.  Write **He, She, It** or **They** in each blank.

1. John won first place. _____ got a blue ribbon.	
2. Janet and Gail rode on a bus. _____ went to visit their grandmother.	
3. Sarah had a birthday party. _____ invited six friends to the party.	
4. The kitten likes to play. _____ likes to tug on shoelaces.	
5. Ed is seven years old. _____ is in the second grade.	

Words That Describe

Name _____

Some words "describe" a person, place or thing.
These words help tell more about a naming word.
Example: The shoe is old.

Read these words that describe.

 the correct word under each picture.

cold	round	funny
light	sad	fat

_____

_____

_____

_____

_____

_____

_____

_____

_____

_____

_____

_____

_____

_____

_____

_____

_____

_____

Match the Describing Word

Match the describing word with the correct picture.

old

soft

hot

sweet

wet

tall

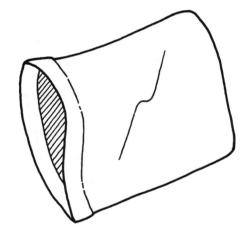

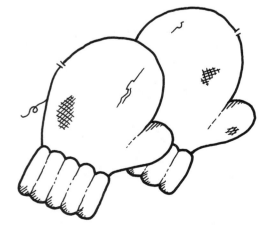

Describing Words

A describing word tells about a noun. It can tell what color, what size, what shape or how many.

 a describing word in each sentence below. Use the word bank to help you.

Word Bank

big   bushy   three
round   green   six

1. A 🐿 has a _____ tail.

2. A 🐞 has _____ legs.

3. The 🐸 will become a _____ frog.

4. A 🦫 has _____ teeth.

5. _____ hang by their tails.

6. An 🦉 has _____ eyes.

What Is It Like?

Describing words tell about a person, place or thing. They can tell how things look, or taste, or sound or feel.

Find the **two** describing words in each sentence below.  them.

1. The white kitten is fluffy.	
2. Two noisy squirrels ran up a tree.	
3. This old book is torn.	
4. The apple was sweet and crisp.	
5. The bright sun is warm on my neck.	
6. Six ducks swam in a round pond.	

78

Which One?

Name _____

Read the two describing words in each box. and the picture they describe.

white		soft	
cold		old	
sad		striped	
wet		short	
furry		round	
small		hard	

What Is It Like?

*these describing words under the correct picture.

sticky	hungry	soft	little
furry	white	fat	big

Corn Crackles

Name _____

Here are some describing words:

sour   furry   sweet   tasty   crisp

tall   crunchy   cloudy   sad   soft

Which four words do you think might best describe
the cereal? ✏ them on the lines on the cereal box.

16 oz.

CORN CRACKLES

Surprise inside!

Puzzle on back!

"A" or "An" ?

The words "a" and "an" help point out a noun. Use "a" before a word that begins with a consonant. Use "an" before a word that begins with a vowel. Example: Trish read **a story**.

It was about **an elephant**.

1. Our class visited _____ farm.

2. We could only stay _____ hour.

3. A man let us pick eggs out of _____ nest.

4. We saw _____ egg that was cracked.

5. We watched _____ lady milk a cow.

6. We got to eat _____ ice cream cone.

82

Color Words

Name _____

Color words can describe things.
Example: Sue has a blue dress.
The banana is yellow.

Use the describing words in the sentences below to help you color the picture.

1. The leaves on the tree are **green**.

2. The tree has **red** apples.

3. A **brown** squirrel sits by the tree.

4. The house is **blue**.

5. **Purple** flowers grow in the yard.

6. **Yellow** birds fly in the sky.

Weather Words

Name _____

Some describing words tell about weather.

 sunny	 cloudy
 rainy	 snowy	 windy

 the correct weather word in each sentence.

1. We can build a on a _____ day.

2. You need an on a _____ day.

3. Your may blow off on a _____ day.

4. You may wear on a _____ day.

5. We may not see the on a _____ day.

Number Words

Number words can be used to describe things.
Number words tell how many.
Example: **Two** ants crawled across the table.

Look at the picture. Read the sentences below. the describing word in each sentence that tells how many.

1. Four spiders hung in the doorway.

2. The witch held three apples.

3. In the window were two jack-o'-lanterns.

4. One cat sat under the table.

5. Five bats hung upside down.

More Describing

Name _____

✎ the describing word in each sentence.
Match each sentence to the correct picture.

1. The girl has new shoes.

2. He saw a long snake.

3. She drew a white duck.

4. The little boy ate a cookie.

5. Three fish swim in the lake.

6. Wagons have round wheels.

Review —
Describing Words

only the fish with describing words.

rug

sunny

loud

big

good

warm

bed

green

quilt

moan

old

hot

Words That Tell Where

Some words tell where.
Example: His shoes are by the bed.

Read the sentence pairs. Match each sentence with
the correct picture.

The dog is in the house.

The dog is out of the house.

The goat is on the bridge.

The goat is under the bridge.

The cat is in front of the tree.

The cat is behind the tree.

The bug crawled through the log.

The bug crawled over the log.

Names of People

The names of people begin with a capital letter.
Example: Mark is my friend.

the names correctly on each child's shirt.
Remember to start each name with a capital letter.

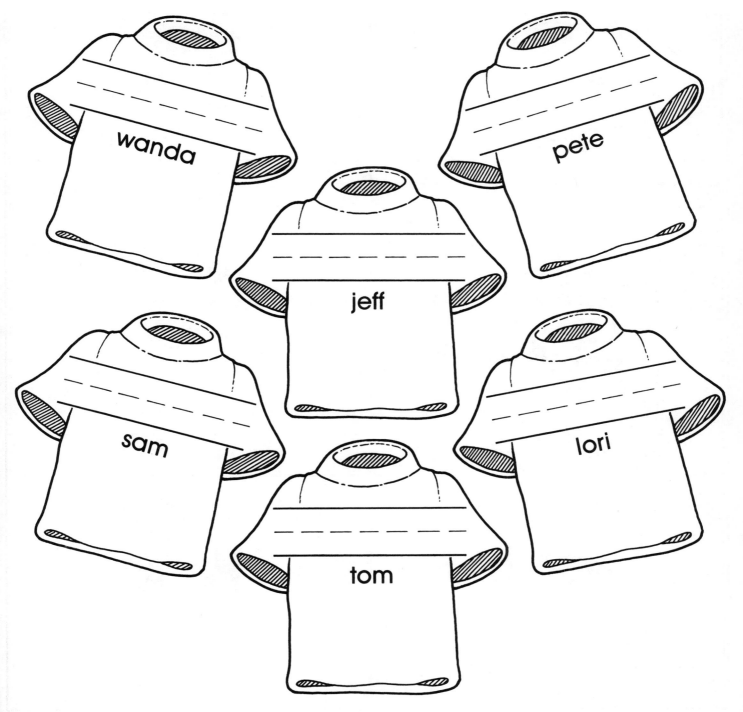

wanda

pete

jeff

sam

lori

tom

Names of People

Name _____

Begin the first and last names of people with capital letters. Example: <u>L</u>ee <u>J</u>ones

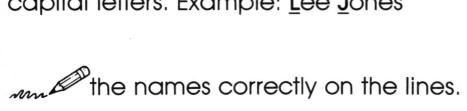 the names correctly on the lines.

_____
- - - - - - - - - - - -
_____
john conley

_____
- - - - - - - - - - - -
_____
tim turner

_____
- - - - - - - - - - - -
_____
jane duncan

_____
- - - - - - - - - - - -
_____
pete warner

_____
- - - - - - - - - - - -
_____
lori boyle

_____
- - - - - - - - - - - -
_____
kate cooper

Names of Pets

Use a capital letter to begin the name of a pet.
Example: My dog is named Duke.

Look at the names on the tags.
the names correctly on the boxes.

Dog Show

fifi

scotty

bandit

pug

rusty

hans

skye

Names of Pets

Name _____

> The name of a pet begins with a capital letter.
> Example: My dog is named Ruff.

Buffy

King

Tara

Poky

Goldie

✏️ the name of the correct pet in each sentence below. Remember to begin each name with a capital.

1. The name of the turtle is _____ .

2. The name of the big dog is _____ .

3. The name of the small dog is _____ .

4. The name of the cat is _____ .

5. The name of the goldfish is _____ .

Book Titles

The first word and every important word in a title begin with a capital letter.
Example:

The Black Cave

✏️ only the books with correct titles.

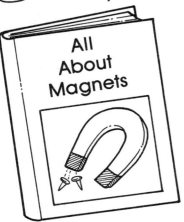

All About Magnets

Abe Lincoln

Ollie Octopus

The Giant and The Elf

Math Magic

Snakes and Lizards

Stamp Collecting

Camping Can Be Fun

Days of the Week

Name _____

Begin the name of each day of the week with a capital letter. Example: Monday

Match the correct letter to each day of the week.	Write the names of the days of the week in order.
S ☐ uesday	_____
T ☐ hursday	_____
T ☐ unday	_____
S ☐ ednesday	_____
W ☐ aturday	_____
F ☐ onday	_____
M ☐ riday	_____

Days of the Week

Name _____

The names of the days of the week begin with capital letters.
Example: Today is **Monday**.
I sleep late on **Saturday**.

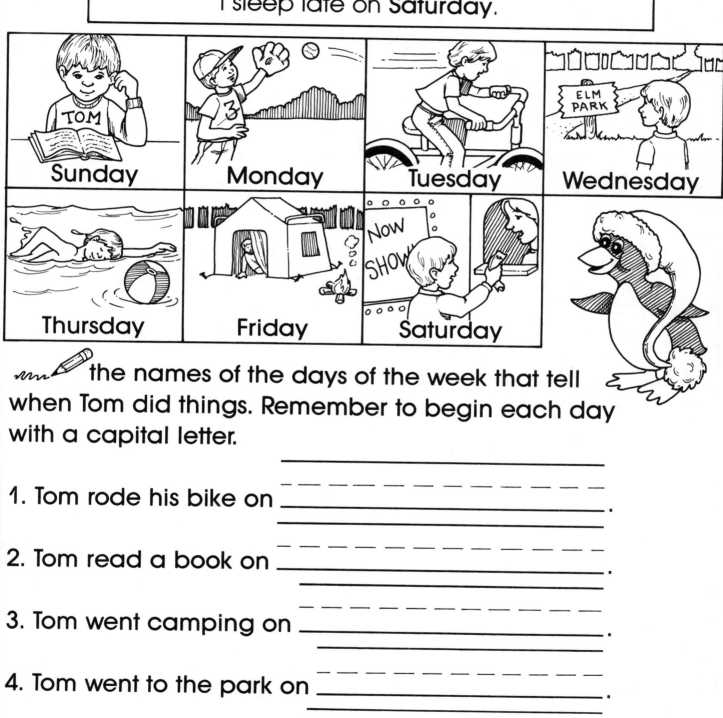

Sunday	Monday	Tuesday	Wednesday
Thursday	Friday	Saturday	

✏ the names of the days of the week that tell when Tom did things. Remember to begin each day with a capital letter.

1. Tom rode his bike on _____ .

2. Tom read a book on _____ .

3. Tom went camping on _____ .

4. Tom went to the park on _____ .

5. Tom went swimming on _____ .

Months of the Year

> The names of the months begin with capital letters. Example: **J**anuary

January	February	March	April
May	June	July	August
September	October	November	December

✏ the name of the correct month on each line.

1. School starts in _____ .

2. Valentine's Day is in _____ .

3. Thanksgiving is in _____ .

4. Father's Day is in _____ .

5. Halloween is in _____ .

Holidays

Begin the name of a holiday with a capital letter.
Example: New Year's Day

Fill in the missing letters. Use the words in the word box to help you. Remember to begin the name of each holiday with a capital letter.

| Halloween | Valentine's Day | Washington's Birthday |
| Thanksgiving | Mother's Day | Fourth of July |

☐ hanksgiving

☐ ashington's ☐ irthday

☐ alentine's ☐ ay

☐ alloween

☐ ourth of ☐ uly

Writing "I"

> Always write the word "I" with a capital letter.
> Example: I can swim.

Read the sentences below.  the word "I."

1. I am six years old.

2. May I eat the ice cream?

3. Phil and I like to ride bikes.

"I" in the sentences below.

1. May _____ read the book?

2. _____ go to school.

3. Rob and _____ are friends.

4. _____ can sing.

5. Am _____ first in line?

Writing "I"

> Always capitalize the first word in a sentence and the word "I." Example: <u>I</u> am seven.

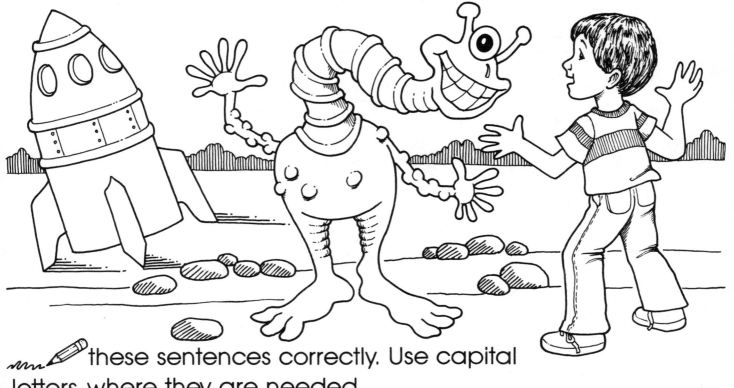

these sentences correctly. Use capital letters where they are needed.

1. i like to pretend.

_____

2. i saw a spaceship land.

_____

3. then i watched a space creature get out.

_____

4. soon i took him home.

_____

5. he and i became friends.

_____

99

Contractions

A contraction is a short way of writing two words.
We use an apostrophe ' in a contraction to
show that a letter or letters have been left out.
Example: I'm = I am

a line from each pair of words to the right
contraction.

he is •   • it's

it is •   • she's

she is •   • he's

they are •   • you're

you are •   • they're

we are •   • I'm

I am •   • we're

"Will" Contractions

Read the contractions in the 🏠.

✏️ the two words that mean the same as the

shortened word.

"will"
contractions

I'll	_____ _____
he'll	_____ _____
they'll	_____ _____
we'll	_____ _____
she'll	_____ _____
you'll	_____ _____

"Not" Contractions

Word Bank

haven't	didn't	isn't
hasn't	don't	can't

Find the correct contraction for each pair of words. ✏️ it on the line.

1. Sally _____ want to get out of bed today.
   did not

2. She _____ ready for school.
   is not

3. She _____ brushed her teeth.
   has not

4. Her friends _____ want to miss the bus.
   do not

5. They _____ time to wait for her.
   have not

6. They _____ be late.
   can not

102

Answer Key

The Alphabet

_____ a line to connect the dots. Follow the letters of the alphabet.

Missing Letters

_____ the missing letters.

a b _c_ d e	f g h _i_ j
k _l_ m n o	_p_ q r s t
u v w x _y_ z	
A _B_ C D E	F G _H_ I J
K L M N _O_	P Q R _S_ T
_U_ V W X Y Z	

What Comes First?

The first letter of each word is used to put words in alphabetical (ABC) order.
Example: <u>a</u>pple, <u>b</u>ee, <u>c</u>ar

_____ the first letter of each word.
_____ the words in alphabetical order.

frog	jar	leaf
baby	dog	shoe
1. baby	1. dog	1. leaf
2. frog	2. jar	2. shoe
wagon	girl	nest
ring	key	hen
1. ring	1. girl	1. hen
2. wagon	2. key	2. nest

ABC Word Trail

Take a trip through the zoo in alphabetical (ABC) order.

Page 1

Page 2

Page 3

Page 4

Grammar IF8729

103

Answer Key

ABC Garden

Mr. Murphy wanted to plant his garden in ABC order.
Read the names of the vegetables in the word box.
Put the vegetables in the correct rows.

corn	tomatoes	lettuce	asparagus	potatoes
onions	beets	radishes	yams	spinach

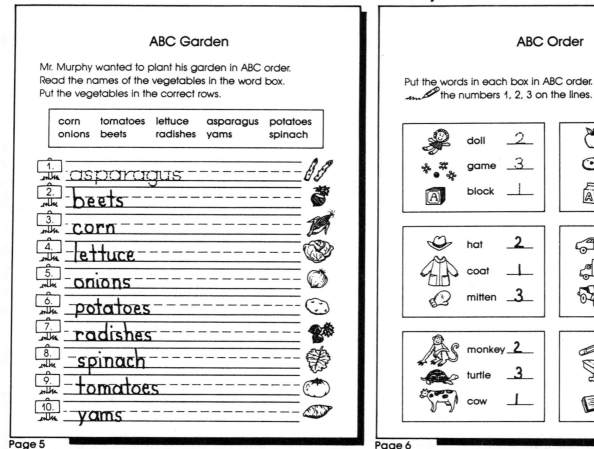

1. asparagus
2. beets
3. corn
4. lettuce
5. onions
6. potatoes
7. radishes
8. spinach
9. tomatoes
10. yams

ABC Order

Put the words in each box in ABC order.
✐ the numbers 1, 2, 3 on the lines.

doll	2		apple	1
game	3		cookie	2
block	1		milk	3

hat	2		car	1
coat	1		truck	3
mitten	3		jeep	2

monkey	2		pencil	3
turtle	3		desk	2
cow	1		book	1

Compound Words

Sometimes two words are put together to make one new word. The new word is called a **compound word**. Example: cow + boy = cowboy

Look at the pictures below. Add the words together and ✐ a new word on the line.

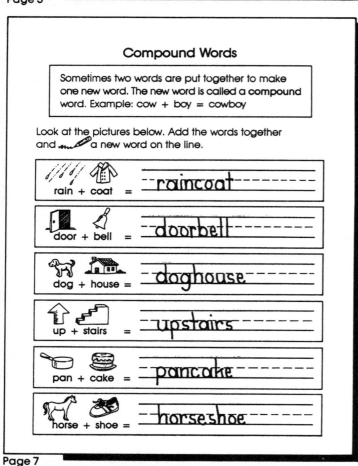

rain + coat = raincoat

door + bell = doorbell

dog + house = doghouse

up + stairs = upstairs

pan + cake = pancake

horse + shoe = horseshoe

Two Words in One

✐ the two words that make up each compound word below.

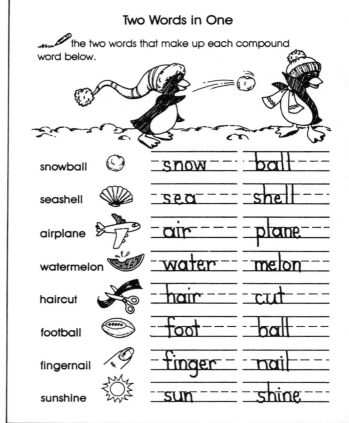

snowball	snow	ball
seashell	sea	shell
airplane	air	plane
watermelon	water	melon
haircut	hair	cut
football	foot	ball
fingernail	finger	nail
sunshine	sun	shine

Answer Key

Writing Compound Words

Read each sentence. ✏ a line under the two words in each sentence that can make a new word. ✏ the compound word on the line.

1. A <u>bird</u> that is <u>black</u> is a **blackbird**.

2. A <u>horse</u> that can <u>race</u> is a **horserace**.

3. A <u>cloth</u> that covers the <u>table</u> is a **tablecloth**.

4. A <u>room</u> where you have a <u>bed</u> is a **bedroom**.

5. A <u>book</u> with a <u>story</u> is a **storybook**.

6. A <u>bowl</u> used to hold <u>fish</u> is a **fishbowl**.

Page 9

Sound Words

Some words tell about sounds and about actions that go with sounds. Example: lightning - crash
owl - hoot

Find a word from the word bank that describes each picture. ✏ the word under the picture.

Word Bank

chirp	pop	crash
bang	boom	gulp

bang   chirp   gulp

crash   boom   pop

Page 10

Sound Riddles

✏ a line from each riddle to the right picture.

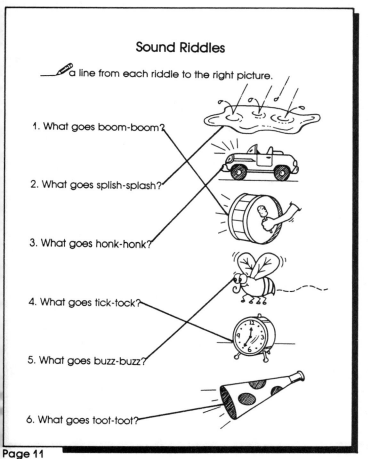

1. What goes boom-boom?

2. What goes splish-splash?

3. What goes honk-honk?

4. What goes tick-tock?

5. What goes buzz-buzz?

6. What goes toot-toot?

Page 11

Finding Opposites

Read each sentence. ✏ the word that means the opposite of the underlined word.

1. The ___ is <u>on</u>.   (off)   hard   wet

2. The ___ is bright at <u>night</u>.   big   hot   (day)

3. The ___ is <u>sad</u>.   go   (happy)   top

4. The ___ is <u>high</u>.   (low)   soft   cold

5. Those ___ look <u>old</u>.   over   (new)   up

6. The ___ is <u>open</u>.   tall   short   (closed)

Page 12

Answer Key

Opposites

Below each word, ✏ a word that means the opposite. Use the word bank to help you.

Word Bank			
lost	down	go	low
left	sad	empty	dry

won	stop	full	happy
lost	_go_	_empty_	_sad_
wet	high	right	up
dry	_low_	_left_	_down_

Matching Opposites

✏ a line to match opposites.

old	back
front	cry
laugh	new
fat	thin
big	night
day	little

Almost Alike

Some words have the same or almost the same meaning.
Example: She is glad.
          She is happy.

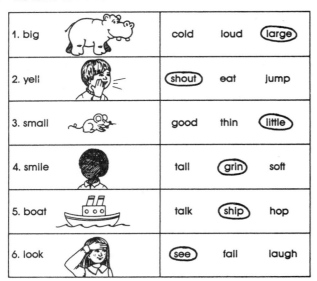

Read the words. ✏ the word that means almost the same as the first word.

1. big		cold	loud	(large)
2. yell		(shout)	eat	jump
3. small		good	thin	(little)
4. smile		tall	(grin)	soft
5. boat		talk	(ship)	hop
6. look		(see)	fall	laugh

Almost Alike

Read the sentences. Find a word in the word bank that means almost the same as the circled word. ✏ it on the line.

Word Bank				
shut	big	start	sleepy	talk

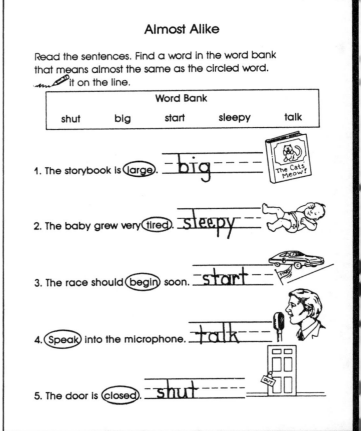

1. The storybook is (large). _big_

2. The baby grew very (tired). _sleepy_

3. The race should (begin) soon. _start_

4. (Speak) into the microphone. _talk_

5. The door is (closed). _shut_

Answer Key

Almost the Same Meaning

Read the words in the word box. ✏ two words under each picture.

rock	start	road	begin	street	stone
shut	sad	talk	unhappy	speak	closed

begin
start

rock
stone

road
street

sad
unhappy

speak
talk

closed
shut

Same or Opposite?

✏ yellow the spaces that have word pairs with opposite meanings.
✏ blue the spaces that have word pairs with the same meanings.

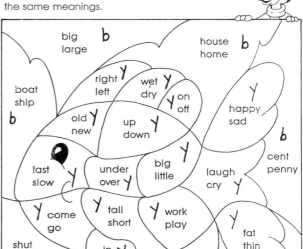

Words That Sound Alike

Words that sound the same may not mean the same or be spelled the same.
Example: I **know** how to read.
         I have **no** pencil.

Read the sentences below. ✏ the correct word on each line.

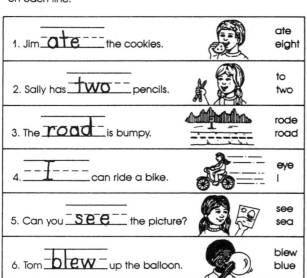

1. Jim **ate** the cookies. — ate / eight
2. Sally has **two** pencils. — to / two
3. The **road** is bumpy. — rode / road
4. **I** can ride a bike. — eye / I
5. Can you **see** the picture? — see / sea
6. Tom **blew** up the balloon. — blew / blue

Words That Sound the Same

Some words sound the same but do not have the same meanings or spellings.
Example: I **know** how to spell.
         I have **no** book.

✏ a word that sounds like each of these but is spelled in a different way. Use the word bank below to help you.

1. blew **blue**
2. road **rode**
3. ate **eight**
4. two **too**
5. some **sum**
6. new **knew**
7. right **write**
8. not **knot**

Word Bank

blue	too	knot	write
sum	rode	eight	knew

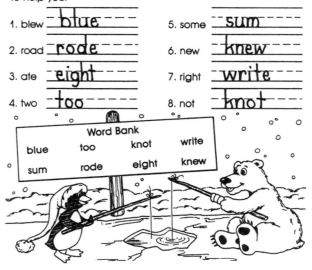

Answer Key

Do They Sound Alike?

only the balloons with words that sound alike.

frog fox

✓ I eye

eye ear

pie pig

✓ right write

✓ sun son

✓ no know

✓ so sew

bat box

✓ one won

Sound Alike Words

the correct word to finish each sentence.

1. Billy went swimming in the (sea, see).
2. The (sun, son) was shining.
3. He saw a boat with a large (sale, sail).
4. Billy and Cindy put sand in a (pail, pale).
5. They (wood, would) like to visit the seashore again.

Sentences

All sentences begin with a capital letter.
Example: The barn is red.

the first word of each sentence. Remember to begin with a capital letter.

1. *Our* _____ class went to the airport.
   (our)
2. *Big* _____ jets were noisy.
   (big)
3. *One* _____ helicopter landed.
   (one)
4. *We* _____ saw some men washing airplanes.
   (we)
5. *The* _____ pilot wore a uniform.
   (the)

Sentence Parts — The Naming Part

A sentence has two parts — the naming part and the action part. The **naming part** tells **whom** or **what** the sentence is about.
Example: **The chimp** rode a bike.

_____ a line under the naming part in each sentence below.

1. <u>Our class</u> had a picnic in the park.
2. <u>Some teachers</u> played ball with us.
3. <u>The hot dogs</u> were good to eat.
4. <u>Big trees</u> grew along the road.
5. <u>A man</u> was jogging.
6. <u>A woman</u> was fishing in the lake.

Answer Key

Writing the Naming Part

Read the naming parts in the tent.
🖉 one of the naming parts to begin each sentence.

1. <u>Todd and Clint</u> went camping.
2. <u>The old green tent</u> was hard to set up.
3. <u>A big wind</u> blew the trees.
4. <u>Black clouds</u> filled the sky.
5. <u>Rain</u> ran off the tent.
6. <u>The campfire</u> went out.

Page 25

Sentence Parts — The Action Part

The action part of a sentence tells what the naming part is doing or did.
Example: Bill throws the ball.

___ a line under the action part in each sentence below.

1. My family <u>walked to the zoo</u>.
2. The seals <u>swam in a pool of water</u>.
3. A monkey <u>climbed a tree</u>.
4. Two big elephants <u>swung their trunks</u>.
5. A striped tiger <u>paced in its cage</u>.
6. The giraffe <u>stretched its long neck</u>.

Page 26

Writing the Action Part

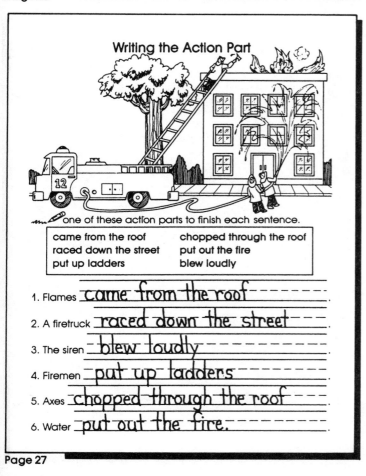

🖉 one of these action parts to finish each sentence.

came from the roof	chopped through the roof
raced down the street	put out the fire
put up ladders	blew loudly

1. Flames <u>came from the roof</u>.
2. A firetruck <u>raced down the street</u>.
3. The siren <u>blew loudly</u>.
4. Firemen <u>put up ladders</u>.
5. Axes <u>chopped through the roof</u>.
6. Water <u>put out the fire.</u>

Page 27

Matching Sentence Parts

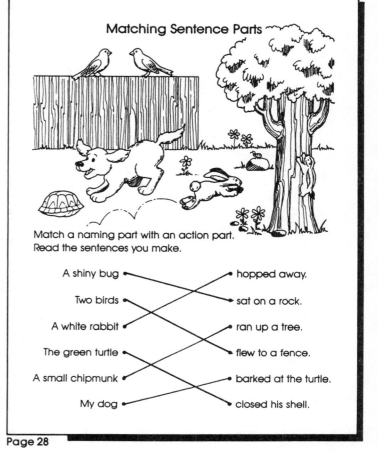

Match a naming part with an action part.
Read the sentences you make.

A shiny bug • • hopped away.
Two birds • • sat on a rock.
A white rabbit • • ran up a tree.
The green turtle • • flew to a fence.
A small chipmunk • • barked at the turtle.
My dog • • closed his shell.

Page 28

Answer Key

Telling Sentences

> Some sentences tell something.
> Telling sentences begin with a capital letter.
> Telling sentences end with a period.
> Example: The bird sings.

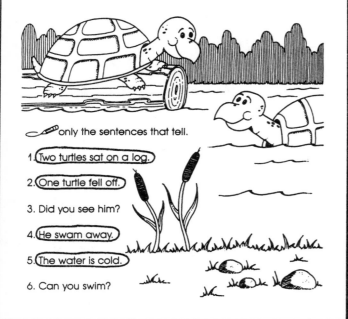

only the sentences that tell.

1. Two turtles sat on a log.
2. One turtle fell off.
3. Did you see him?
4. He swam away.
5. The water is cold.
6. Can you swim?

Page 29

A Statement

> Some sentences tell something.
> They are called statements.
> A statement begins with a capital letter.
> A statement ends with a period.
> Example: [T]he teacher helped the child[.]

these statements correctly.

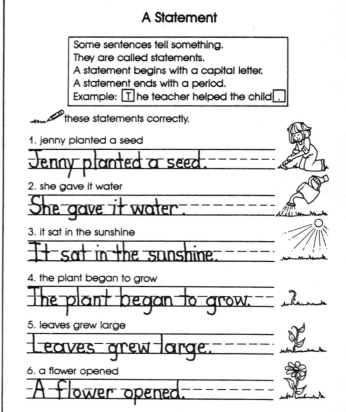

1. jenny planted a seed

Jenny planted a seed.

2. she gave it water

She gave it water.

3. it sat in the sunshine

It sat in the sunshine.

4. the plant began to grow

The plant began to grow.

5. leaves grew large

Leaves grew large.

6. a flower opened

A flower opened.

Page 30

Writing a Telling Sentence

the telling sentences below. Begin each sentence with a capital letter and end with a period.

1. dinosaurs lived long ago

Dinosaurs lived long ago.

2. many were very big

Many were very big.

3. some dinosaurs ate plants

Some dinosaurs ate plants.

4. all the dinosaurs died out

All the dinosaurs died out.

5. no one is sure why

No one is sure why.

Page 31

Asking Sentences

> Some sentences ask something.
> An asking sentence is called a question.
> A question begins with a capital letter.
> A question ends with a question mark.
> Example: What is your name?

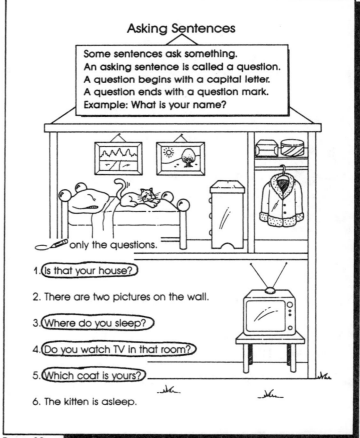

only the questions.

1. Is that your house?
2. There are two pictures on the wall.
3. Where do you sleep?
4. Do you watch TV in that room?
5. Which coat is yours?
6. The kitten is asleep.

Page 32

Answer Key

A Question

Some sentences ask something.
An asking sentence is called a question.
A question begins with a capital letter.
A question ends with a question mark.
Example: [H]ow tall are you [?]

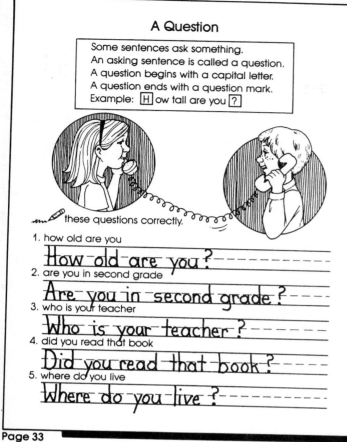

✏ these questions correctly.

1. how old are you

How old are you?

2. are you in second grade

Are you in second grade?

3. who is your teacher

Who is your teacher?

4. did you read that book

Did you read that book?

5. where do you live

Where do you live?

Writing a Question

✏ the first word of each question below.
Remember to begin with a capital letter. End each
question with a question mark.

1. Is (is) that your boat?

2. Did (did) you catch that fish?

3. How (how) much does it weigh?

4. Will (will) you eat it?

5. Did (did) you fish with worms?

6. Is (is) the water cold?

Statement or Question?

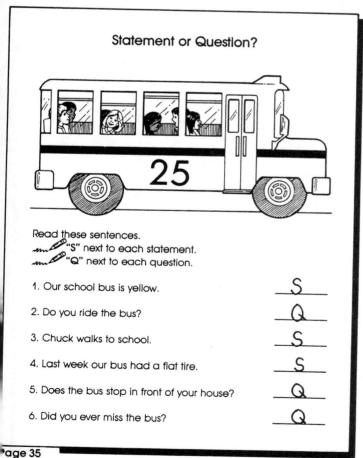

Read these sentences.
✏ "S" next to each statement.
✏ "Q" next to each question.

1. Our school bus is yellow.　　　　S

2. Do you ride the bus?　　　　Q

3. Chuck walks to school.　　　　S

4. Last week our bus had a flat tire.　　　　S

5. Does the bus stop in front of your house?　　　　Q

6. Did you ever miss the bus?　　　　Q

Period or Question Mark?

Put a period or question mark in each box below.

1. Ryan and Emily had a picnic [.]

2. They fed bread to the ducks [.]

3. Do you think the ducks will fly away [?]

4. Will they come back next summer [?]

5. Ants crawled on the table [.]

6. Are they hungry, too [?]

Answer Key

Period or Question Mark?

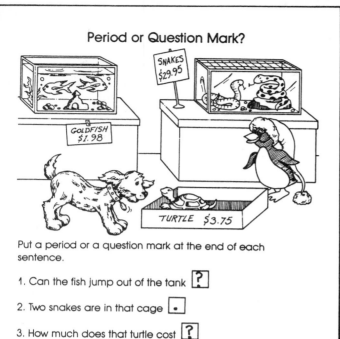

Put a period or a question mark at the end of each sentence.

1. Can the fish jump out of the tank [?]

2. Two snakes are in that cage [.]

3. How much does that turtle cost [?]

4. Yes, I already have a dog [.]

5. His name is King [.]

6. Do you have a dog [?]

Sentence Sense

> The words in a sentence must be in an order that makes sense.

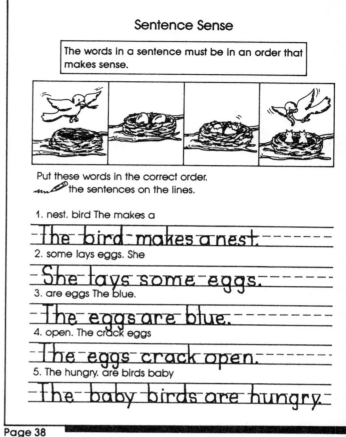

Put these words in the correct order.
✏ the sentences on the lines.

1. nest. bird The makes a

The bird makes a nest.

2. some lays eggs. She

She lays some eggs.

3. are eggs The blue.

The eggs are blue.

4. open. The crack eggs

The eggs crack open.

5. The hungry. are birds baby

The baby birds are hungry

Scrambled Sentences

Unscramble these sentences. ✏ the sentences on the lines.

1. dancing. Little dogs are

Little dogs are dancing.

2. balloons. six has man The

The man has six balloons.

3. clown big The has feet.

The clown has big feet.

4. plays A seal a song.

A seal plays a song.

5. pull monkeys Two a wagon.

Two monkeys pull a wagon.

Word Order

> To make sense, words in a sentence must be in order.

Make a sentence by putting each group of words in the correct order.

1. watched a parade. We

We watched a parade.

2. tricks. did clown A

A clown did tricks.

3. a horse. man A rode

A man rode a horse.

4. lions Big in cage. a were

Big lions were in a cage.

5. marched band by. A

A band marched by.

112

Answer Key

Word Order

Changing the order of the words in a sentence may change the meaning.
Example: The dog chased the cat.
               The cat chased the dog.

Read the sentence pairs.
the sentence that goes with the picture.

(The boy hit the ball.) The ball hit the boy.	
The giant watched the elf. (The elf watched the giant.)	
The teacher read to the girl. (The girl read to the teacher.)	
(The baby laughed at the father.) The father laughed at the baby.	
The frog jumped over the rabbit. (The rabbit jumped over the frog.)	

Jellybean Jumble

The words in each jar are mixed up. Put them in order to make sense. ✏️ the sentences.

We, ball, played, today → **We played ball today.**

Sally, base, first, played → **Sally played first base.**

was, the, Bob, pitcher. → **Bob was the pitcher.**

homerun., Sue, a, hit → **Sue hit a homerun.**

won, Our, the, game., team → **Our team won the game.**

Naming Words

A naming word names a person, place or thing.
Example: person—nurse, boy
         place —park, store
         thing —drum, tree

In the word box below, ✏️ only the words that name a person, place or thing.

(teacher)	(zoo)	(dog)	(hat)	(library)
runs	is	(cowboy)	the	up

Use the naming words you circled to label each picture below.

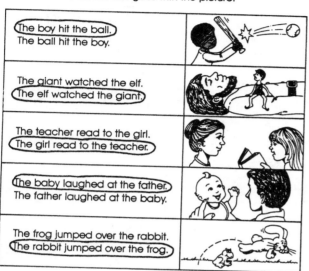

hat   library   teacher

dog   cowboy   zoo

Nouns

A noun is a naming word.
A noun names a person, place or thing.
For example: person: nurse
              place: town
              thing: tree

Find two nouns in each sentence below.
✏️ them.

1. The (pig) has a curly (tail.)	
2. The (hen) is sitting on her (nest)	
3. A (horse) is in the (barn.)	
4. The (goat) has (horns.)	
5. The (cow) has a (calf)	
6. The (farmer) is painting the (fence)	

113

Answer Key

Words That Name Things

tree

sun

barn

ducks

horse

pig   girl   boy   farmer

Read the naming words below. ✏️ the correct naming word for each picture of a person, place or thing.

barn	farmer	pig
boy	tree	horse
girl	ducks	sun

Person, Place or Thing

✏️ these naming words in the correct box.

girl	park	truck
vase	leaf	fireman
fish	doctor	zoo
school	store	ball
man	library	baby

Person

girl   man
doctor   fireman
baby

Place

school   park
store   library
zoo

Thing

vase   fish
leaf   truck
ball

More Naming

✏️ the correct naming word in each sentence.

ducks	dog	sun
boys	tree	bird

1. A big __tree__ grows in the park.

2. The __sun__ is in the sky.

3. A __dog__ digs a hole.

4. Three __ducks__ swim in the water.

5. A __bird__ sits on her nest.

6. Two __boys__ fly a kite.

Person, Place or Thing

✏️ the correct noun in each sentence. Use the picture and the word bank to help you.

Word Bank		
apple	clock	hand
books	chalkboard	children

1. The __children__ are in school.

2. A round __clock__ is on the wall.

3. Tim is writing on the __chalkboard__.

4. One girl is raising her __hand__.

5. There are __books__ on the shelves.

6. The teacher has an __apple__ on her desk.

Answer Key

Scrambled Nouns

Unscramble the letters. ✏ the noun on the line.

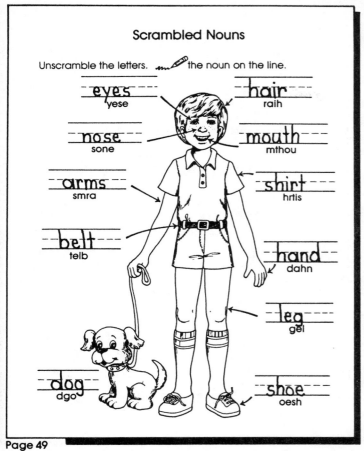

eyes — yese

hair — raih

nose — sone

mouth — mthou

arms — smra

shirt — hrtis

belt — telb

hand — dahn

leg — gel

dog — dgo

shoe — oesh

Naming More Than One

Some words name one person, place or thing.
Example: balloon, girl, egg
Some words name more than one person, place or thing. We often add "s" to a word to make it show more than one.
Example: balloons, girls, eggs

Read the words. Draw a ✏ around the word that tells about the picture.

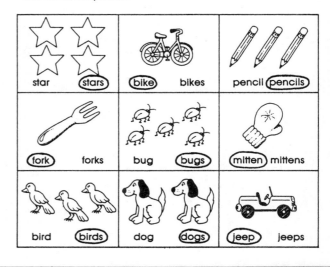

star **(stars)**	**(bike)** bikes	pencil **(pencils)**
(fork) forks	bug **(bugs)**	**(mitten)** mittens
bird **(birds)**	dog **(dogs)**	**(jeep)** jeeps

One or More Than One?

✏ the correct word under each picture.

dish **(dishes)**	**(car)** cars	frog **(frogs)**
(hat) hats	glass **(glasses)**	**(shirt)** shirts
cloud **(clouds)**	wheel **(wheels)**	**(church)** churches

One or More Than One?

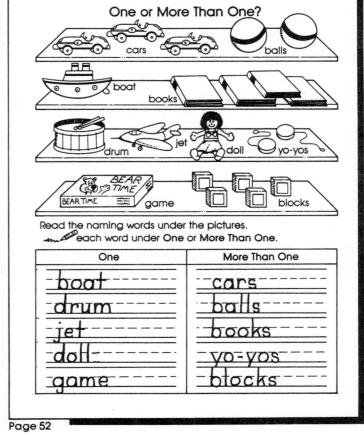

cars balls boat books drum jet doll yo-yos game blocks

Read the naming words under the pictures.
✏ each word under One or More Than One.

One	More Than One
boat	cars
drum	balls
jet	books
doll	yo-yos
game	blocks

Answer Key

Adding "s"

A plural word means more than one. We add "s" to most nouns to make a plural.
Example: Sid has **one dog**.
Jerry has **two dogs**.

✏️ the plural form of the words below.

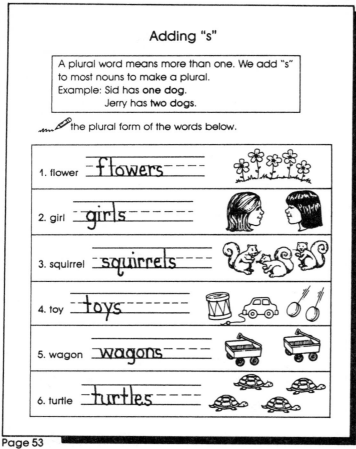

1. flower __flowers__
2. girl __girls__
3. squirrel __squirrels__
4. toy __toys__
5. wagon __wagons__
6. turtle __turtles__

Page 53

Adding "es"

A plural word means more than one. We usually add "es" to words that end in **x, s, ss, sh** or **ch**.
Example: He filled **one box** with sand.
He filled **four boxes** with sand.

✏️ the plural form of each word below.

1. peach __peaches__
2. brush __brushes__
3. fox __foxes__
4. dress __dresses__
5. bus __buses__
6. witch __witches__

Page 54

Plural Review

Decide if the words mean **one** or **more than one**.
✏️ the words on the fish in the correct tank.

| kites | star | chick | foxes |
| mitten | cats | matches | lunch |

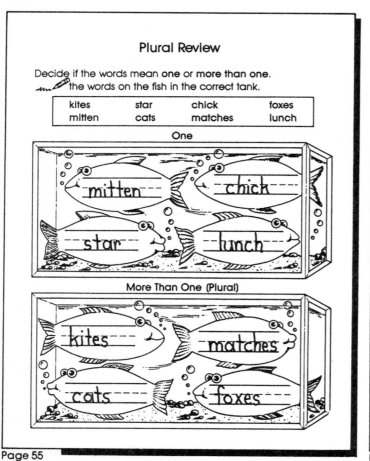

One

mitten   chick
star   lunch

More Than One (Plural)

kites   matches
cats   foxes

Page 55

Adding " 's"

Add " 's" to a noun to show who or what **owns** something.
Example: The dog belongs to Larry.
It is Larry's dog.

✏️ the correct word under each picture.

The ___ nose is big.
clown   clowns   (clown's)

This is ___ coat.
Bettys   (Betty's)   Betty

I know ___ brother.
(Burt's)   Burt   Burts

The ___ hat is pretty.
girls   girl   (girl's)

That is the ___ ball.
(kitten's)   kitten   kittens

My ___ shoe is missing.
sisters   sister   (sister's)

The ___ coach is Mr. Hall.
teams   (team's)   team

The ___ cover is torn.
(book's)   books   book

Page 56

Grammar IF8729

116

© 1990 Instructional Fair, Inc.

Answer Key

Ownership

An " 's" at the end of a word shows ownership.

Read the sentence pairs. Finish the second sentence to show ownership. The first one has been done for you.

1. The red wagon belongs to Mike. It is ___Mike's___ red wagon.	
2. The fur of the rabbit is soft. The __rabbit's__ fur is soft.	
3. The name of my friend is Donna. My __friend's__ name is Donna.	
4. The tail of the pig is curly. The __pig's__ tail is curly.	
5. The tire of the bike is flat. The __bike's__ tire is flat.	
6. That mitten belongs to Jane. That is __Jane's__ mitten.	

Action Words

An action word tells what a person or thing can do.
Example: Fred kicks the ball.

Read the action words below. ✏ the ones you can do.

jump		skate	
swim		sleep	
sing		hop	
talk		read	

Match the Action Word!

Find the action word in each sentence. ✏ it.
✏ a line to match each sentence with the correct picture.

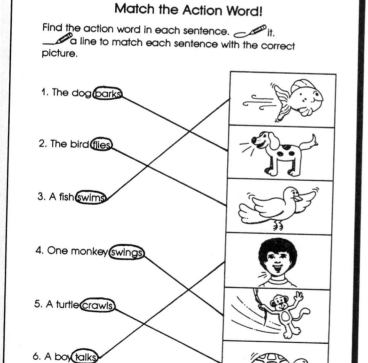

1. The dog (barks)
2. The bird (flies)
3. A fish (swims)
4. One monkey (swings)
5. A turtle (crawls)
6. A boy (talks)

Verbs

A verb is an action word. A verb tells what a person or thing does or did.
Example: Jane reads a book.

Find the verb in each sentence below and ✏ it.

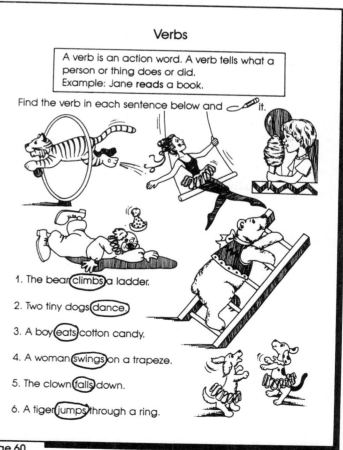

1. The bear (climbs) a ladder.
2. Two tiny dogs (dance.)
3. A boy (eats) cotton candy.
4. A woman (swings) on a trapeze.
5. The clown (falls) down.
6. A tiger (jumps) through a ring.

117

Answer Key

What a Person or Thing Can Do

Read the action words in the word box.
✏ the correct word under each picture.

eat	laugh	swing
build	sit	throw

build   laugh

sit   swing

throw   eat

Writing Verns

Word Bank		
beat	sang	told
danced	sat	wore

✏ a verb in each sentence below. Use the word bank to help you.

1. The boys and girls **sat** around the campfire.

2. They **sang** songs.

3. Brian **beat** a drum.

4. Jerry and Helen **wore** Indian costumes.

5. They **danced** around the campfire.

6. The teacher **told** stories.

More Action Words

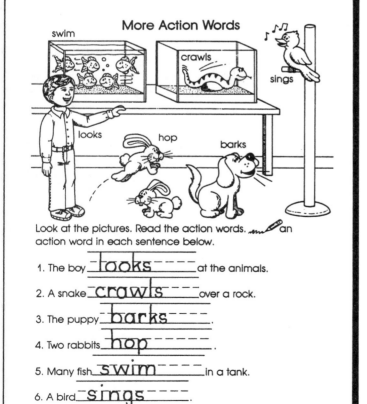

Look at the pictures. Read the action words. ✏ an action word in each sentence below.

1. The boy **looks** at the animals.

2. A snake **crawls** over a rock.

3. The puppy **barks**.

4. Two rabbits **hop**.

5. Many fish **swim** in a tank.

6. A bird **sings**.

Using Is and Are

Use "is" when talking about one person or thing.
Use "are" when talking about more than one.
Example: The girl is reading.
     The girls are reading.

✏ "is" or "are" in the sentences below.

1. The baby **is** sleeping.

2. Cookies **are** good to eat.

3. Apples **are** sweet and crisp.

4. A boy **is** painting a picture.

5. The ducks **are** in the pond.

6. The girl **is** riding her bike.

Answer Key

Using "Is," "Are" and "Am"

> Use "is" and "are" to tell about now.
> Use "is" to tell about one person or thing.
> Use "are" to tell about more than one.
> Use "are" with the word "you."
> Use "am" with the word "I."

"is," "are" or "am" in each sentence below.

1. The lake **is** deep.

2. I **am** fishing.

3. Sally **is** baiting a hook.

4. Dan and Chuck **are** coming to our cabin.

5. We **are** going to cook the fish for dinner.

6. You **are** invited, too.

Page 65

In the Past

> A verb can tell about something that happened in the past. Some verbs add "ed" to tell about the past.
> Example: Today, Tara and Jim **walk** to school.
>   Yesterday, Tara and Jim **walked** to school.

the correct verb in each sentence.

1. Last week, I **played** in the park.
   (play, played)

2. Yesterday, I **fished** in the lake.
   (fish, fished)

3. Today, I will **help** Dad.
   (help, helped)

4. I **like** to help Dad.
   (like, liked)

5. My sisters **cleaned** their room two hours ago.
   (clean, cleaned)

6. Now they **help** Dad, too.
   (help, helped)

Page 66

Now or In the Past?

these verbs in the correct Time Machine.

| play | pull | barked | jumped | danced |
| looked | laugh | walk | listen | lived |

Now
play
pull
laugh
walk
listen

In the Past
looked
barked
jumped
danced
lived

Page 67

Using "Was" and "Were"

> Use "was" and "were" to tell about something that happened in the past.
> Use "was" to tell about **one** person or thing.
> Use "were" to tell about **more than one** person or thing.
> Always use "were" with the word "you."

"was" or "were" in each sentence below.

1. Lois **was** in the second grade last year.

2. She **was** eight years old.

3. Carmen and Judy **were** friends.

4. They **were** on the same soccer team.

5. I **was** on the team, too.

6. You **were** too young to play.

Page 68

Answer Key

Using "Give," "Gives" and "Gave"

Use "give" and "gives" to tell about now.
Use "gave" to tell about the past.

"give," "gives" or "gave" in each sentence below.

1. Trisha **gave** a party last week.
2. Please **give** me the book.
3. I **give** my dog some water every day.
4. Jill **gave** the jacket to me yesterday.
5. She **gives** me a turn each day.
6. The teacher always **gives** a test on Friday.

Page 69

Using "See," "Sees" and "Saw"

Use "see" or "sees" to tell about now.
Use "saw" to tell about the past.

"see," "sees" or "saw" in each sentence below.

1. I **see** the picture Tom is painting now.
2. He **saw** the bird at the zoo last week.
3. Betsy **sees** something out the window now.
4. She **saw** a rainbow yesterday.
5. We **see** clouds in the sky today.
6. Last week, I **saw** a cloud shaped like a pig.

Page 70

Verb Review

only the leaves that have verbs.

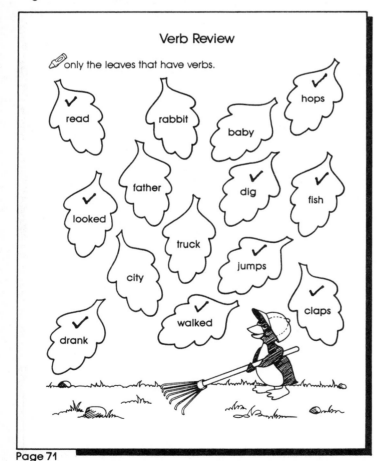

read ✓, rabbit, baby, hops ✓, looked ✓, father, dig ✓, fish ✓, truck, city, jumps ✓, drank ✓, walked ✓, claps ✓

Page 71

Review — Naming Words and Action Words

the spaces with naming words green.
the spaces with action words pink.

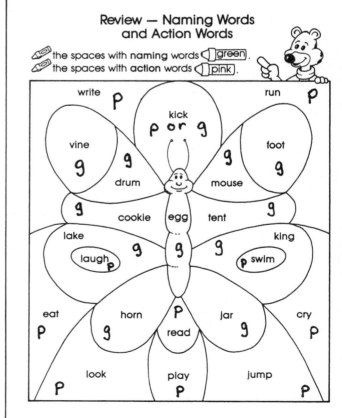

write p, run p, kick p or g, vine g, drum g, foot g, mouse g, cookie g, egg g, tent g, lake, laugh p, g, g, king, swim p, eat p, horn g, read p, jar g, cry p, look p, play p, jump p

Page 72

Answer Key

Review — Nouns and Verbs

one noun and one verb under each picture. Use the word bank to help you.

Word Bank			
skate	leaves	fall	dog
flies	girls	jet	digs
sleeps	hop	baby	boys

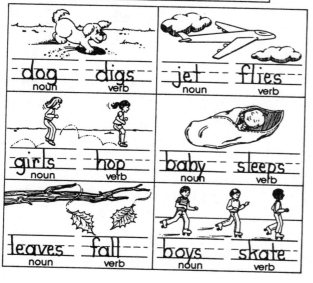

dog (noun) digs (verb) — jet (noun) flies (verb)

girls (noun) hop (verb) — baby (noun) sleeps (verb)

leaves (noun) fall (verb) — boys (noun) skate (verb)

Page 73

In Place of a Noun

The words "he," "she," "it" and "they" can be used in place of a noun.
Example: Jane caught the ball.
She caught the ball.

Read the sentence pairs. He, She, It or They in each blank.

1. John won first place.
   He got a blue ribbon.

2. Janet and Gail rode on a bus.
   They went to visit their grandmother.

3. Sarah had a birthday party.
   She invited six friends to the party.

4. The kitten likes to play.
   It likes to tug on shoelaces.

5. Ed is seven years old.
   He is in the second grade.

Page 74

Words That Describe

Some words "describe" a person, place or thing. These words help tell more about a naming word.
Example: The shoe is old.

Read these words that describe.
the correct word under each picture.

| cold | round | funny |
| light | sad | fat |

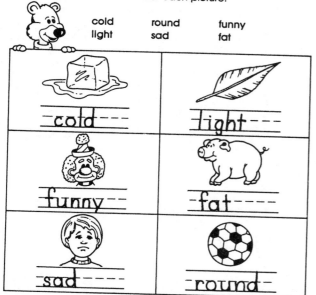

cold — light

funny — fat

sad — round

Page 75

Match the Describing Word

Match the describing word with the correct picture.

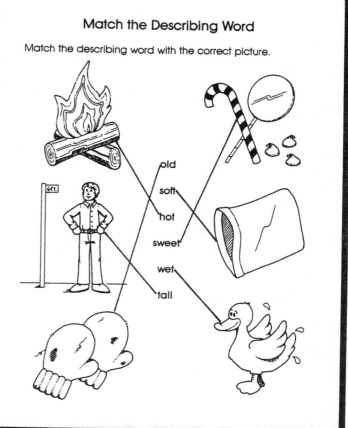

old
soft
hot
sweet
wet
tall

Page 76

Answer Key

Describing Words

A describing word tells about a noun. It can tell what color, what size, what shape or how many.

✏ a describing word in each sentence below. Use the word bank to help you.

Word Bank
big   bushy   three
round   green   six

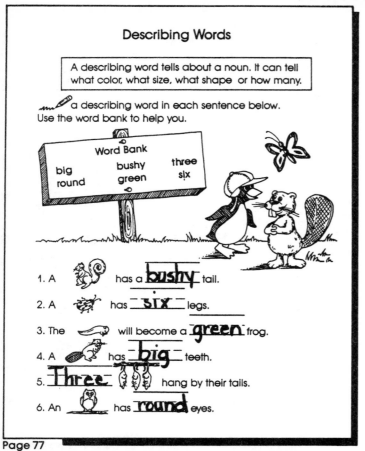

1. A 🐿 has a **bushy** tail.
2. A 🐛 has **six** legs.
3. The 🐛 will become a **green** frog.
4. A 🦫 has **big** teeth.
5. **Three** 🦇🦇🦇 hang by their tails.
6. An 🦉 has **round** eyes.

What Is It Like?

Describing words tell about a person, place or thing. They can tell how things look, or taste, or sound or feel.

Find the **two** describing words in each sentence below. ✏ them.

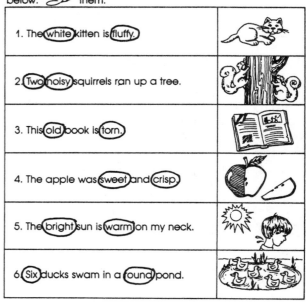

1. The (white) kitten is (fluffy).	
2. (Two) (noisy) squirrels ran up a tree.	
3. This (old) book is (torn).	
4. The apple was (sweet) and (crisp).	
5. The (bright) sun is (warm) on my neck.	
6. (Six) ducks swam in a (round) pond.	

Which One?

Read the two describing words in each box. ✏ and ✏ the picture they describe.

white / cold
soft / old
sad / wet
striped / short
furry / small
round / hard

What Is It Like?

✏ these describing words under the correct picture.

sticky   hungry   soft   little
furry   white   fat   big

sticky   furry
hungry   white
fat   soft
big   little

Answer Key

Corn Crackles

Here are some describing words:

sour   furry   sweet   tasty   crisp
tall   crunchy   cloudy   sad   soft

Which four words do you think might best describe the cereal? ✏️ them on the lines on the cereal box.

16 oz.

CORN CRACKLES

Surprise inside!

crunchy
sweet
tasty
crisp

Puzzle on back!

A or An?

The words "a" and "an" help point out a noun. Use "a" before a word that begins with a consonant. Use "an" before a word that begins with a vowel. Example: Trish read a story.
                    It was about an elephant.

1. Our class visited __a__ farm.

2. We could only stay __an__ hour.

3. A man let us pick eggs out of __a__ nest.

4. We saw __an__ egg that was cracked.

5. We watched __a__ lady milk a cow.

6. We got to eat __an__ ice cream cone.

Color Words

Color words can describe things.
Example: Sue has a blue dress.
          The banana is yellow.

Use the describing words in the sentences below to help you color the picture.

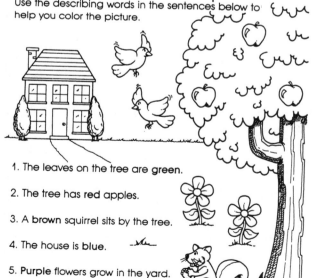

1. The leaves on the tree are green.

2. The tree has red apples.

3. A brown squirrel sits by the tree.

4. The house is blue.

5. Purple flowers grow in the yard.

6. Yellow birds fly in the sky.

Weather Words

Some describing words tell about weather.

sunny   cloudy

rainy   snowy   windy

✏️ the correct weather word in each sentence.

1. We can build a ⛄ on a __snowy__ day.

2. You need an ☂ on a __rainy__ day.

3. Your 🎩 may blow off on a __windy__ day.

4. You may wear 🕶 on a __sunny__ day.

5. We may not see the ☁ on a __cloudy__ day.

Grammar IF8729

123

© 1990 Instructional Fair, Inc.

Answer Key

Number Words

Number words can be used to describe things.
Number words tell how many.
Example: **Two** ants crawled across the table.

Look at the picture. Read the sentences below.
✏ the describing word in each sentence that
tells how many.

1. (Four) spiders hung in the doorway.

2. The witch held (three) apples.

3. In the window were (two) jack-o'-lanterns.

4. (One) cat sat under the table.

5. (Five) bats hung upside down.

More Describing

✏ the describing word in each sentence.
Match each sentence to the correct picture.

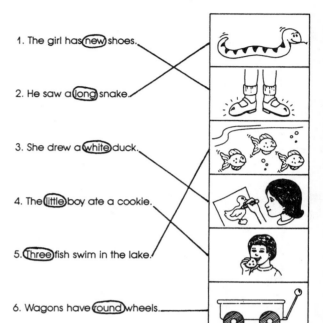

1. The girl has (new) shoes.

2. He saw a (long) snake.

3. She drew a (white) duck.

4. The (little) boy ate a cookie.

5. (Three) fish swim in the lake.

6. Wagons have (round) wheels.

Review — Describing Words

✏ only the fish with describing words.

Words That Tell Where

Some words tell where.
Example: His shoes are by the bed.

Read the sentence pairs. Match each sentence with
the correct picture.

The dog is in the house.

The dog is out of the house.

The goat is on the bridge.

The goat is under the bridge.

The cat is in front of the tree.

The cat is behind the tree.

The bug crawled through the log.

The cug crawled over the log.

Answer Key

Names of People

The names of people begin with a capital letter.
Example: Mark is my friend.

✏ the names correctly on each child's shirt.
Remember to start each name with a capital letter.

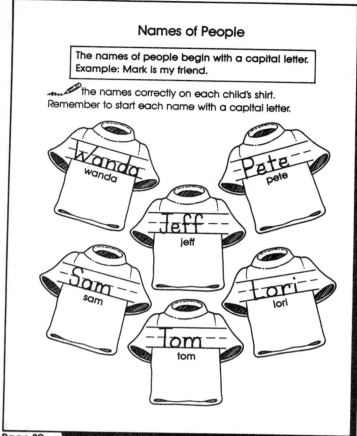

Wanda — wanda
Pete — pete
Jeff — jeff
Sam — sam
Lori — lori
Tom — tom

Names of People

Begin the first and last names of people with capital letters. Example: Lee Jones

✏ the names correctly on the lines.

John Conley	Tim Turner
john conley	tim turner
Jane Duncan	Pete Warner
jane duncan	pete warner
Lori Boyle	Kate Cooper
lori boyle	kate cooper

Names of Pets

Use a capital letter to begin the name of a pet.
Example: My dog is named Duke.

Look at the names on the tags.
✏ the names correctly on the boxes.

Dog Show

fifi — Fifi
scotty — Scotty
bandit — Bandit
pug — Pug
hans — Hans
rusty — Rusty
skye — Skye

Names of Pets

The name of a pet begins with a capital letter.
Example: My dog is named Ruff.

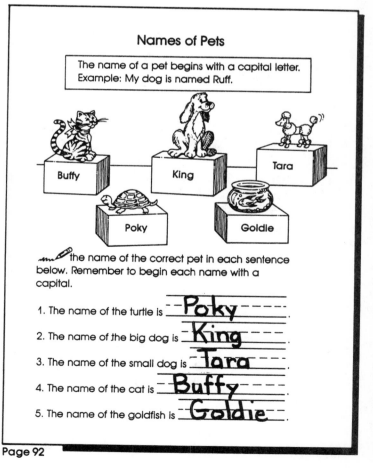

Buffy   King   Tara   Poky   Goldie

✏ the name of the correct pet in each sentence below. Remember to begin each name with a capital.

1. The name of the turtle is __Poky__
2. The name of the big dog is __King__
3. The name of the small dog is __Tara__
4. The name of the cat is __Buffy__
5. The name of the goldfish is __Goldie__

Answer Key

Book Titles

The first word and every important word in a title begin with a capital letter.
Example:

The Black Cave

✏ only the books with correct titles.

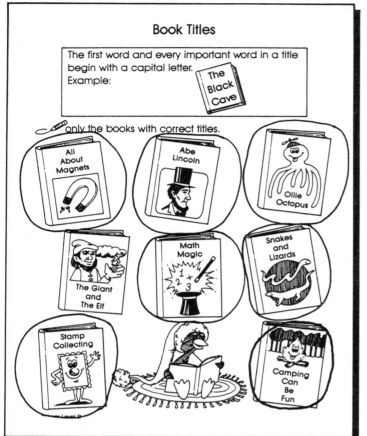

All About Magnets

Abe Lincoln

Ollie Octopus

The Giant and The Elf

Math Magic

Snakes and Lizards

Stamp Collecting

Camping Can Be Fun

Days of the Week

Begin the name of each day of the week with a capital letter. Example: Monday

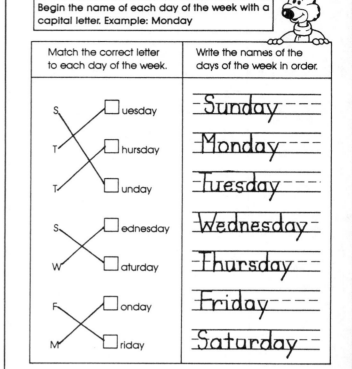

Match the correct letter to each day of the week.	Write the names of the days of the week in order.
S. ☐ uesday	*Sunday*
T. ☐ hursday	*Monday*
T. ☐ unday	*Tuesday*
S. ☐ ednesday	*Wednesday*
W. ☐ aturday	*Thursday*
F. ☐ onday	*Friday*
M. ☐ riday	*Saturday*

Days of the Week

The names of the days of the week begin with capital letters.
Example: Today is **Monday**.
I sleep late on **Saturday**.

Sunday Monday Tuesday Wednesday

Thursday Friday Saturday

✏ the names of the days of the week that tell when Tom did things. Remember to begin each day with a capital letter.

1. Tom rode his bike on *Tuesday*.

2. Tom read a book on *Sunday*.

3. Tom went camping on *Friday*.

4. Tom went to the park on *Wednesday*.

5. Tom went swimming on *Thursday*.

Months of the Year

The names of the months begin with capital letters. Example: January

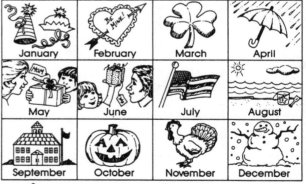

January	February	March	April
May	June	July	August
September	October	November	December

✏ the name of the correct month on each line.

1. School starts in *September*.

2. Valentine's Day is in *February*.

3. Thanksgiving is in *November*.

4. Father's Day is in *June*.

5. Halloween is in *October*.

Answer Key

Holidays

Begin the name of a holiday with a capital letter.
Example: New Year's Day

Fill in the missing letters. Use the words in the word box to help you. Remember to begin the name of each holiday with a capital letter.

| Halloween | Valentine's Day | Washington's Birthday |
| Thanksgiving | Mother's Day | Fourth of July |

[T] hanksgiving   [W] ashington's [B] irthday

[V] alentine's [D] ay   [H] alloween

[F] ourth of [J] uly

Writing "I"

Always write the word "I" with a capital letter.
Example: I can swim.

Read the sentences below. ✏ the word "I."

1. ⓘ am six years old.

2. May ⓘ eat the ice cream?

3. Phil and ⓘ like to ride bikes.

✏ "I" in the sentences below.

1. May I read the book?

2. I go to school.

3. Rob and I are friends.

4. I can sing.

5. Am I first in line?

Writing "I"

Always capitalize the first word in a sentence and the word "I." Example: I am seven.

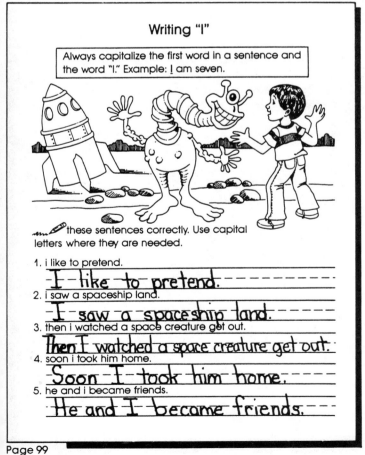

✏ these sentences correctly. Use capital letters where they are needed.

1. i like to pretend.

I like to pretend.

2. i saw a spaceship land.

I saw a spaceship land.

3. then i watched a space creature get out.

Then I watched a space creature get out.

4. soon i took him home.

Soon I took him home.

5. he and i became friends.

He and I became friends.

Contractions

A contraction is a short way of writing two words. We use an apostrophe ' in a contraction to show that a letter or letters have been left out.
Example: I'm = I am

✏ a line from each pair of words to the right contraction.

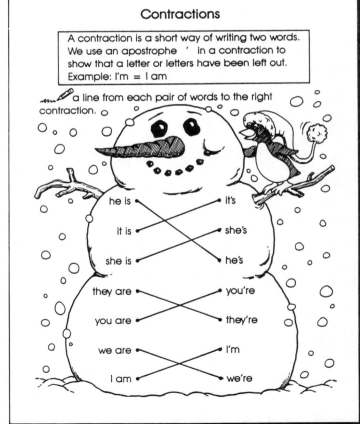

he is   it's
it is   she's
she is   he's

they are   you're
you are   they're
we are   I'm
I am   we're

"Will" Contractions

Read the contractions in the 🏠.
✏️ the two words that mean the same as the shortened word.

"will" contractions

I'll	I will
he'll	he will
they'll	they will
we'll	we will
she'll	she will
you'll	you will

Page 101

"Not" Contractions

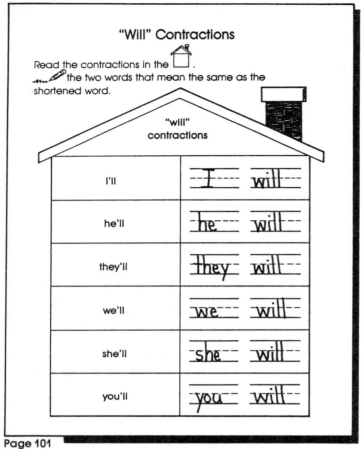

Word Bank

haven't	didn't	isn't
hasn't	don't	can't

Find the correct contraction for each pair of words. ✏️ it on the line.

1. Sally **didn't** want to get out of bed today.
   did not

2. She **isn't** ready for school.
   is not

3. She **hasn't** brushed her teeth.
   has not

4. Her friends **don't** want to miss the bus.
   do not

5. They **haven't** time to wait for her.
   have not

6. They **can't** be late.
   can not

Page 102

About the book . . .

This book offers a wide variety of activities that provide a knowledge of the "rules and regulations" of proper English usage. Some of the basic skills addressed are: ABC order, synonyms, antonyms, homonyms, parts of speech, plurals, verb tense, punctuation, sentences, possession, etc.
Illustrated to enhance student motivation, these activities are packed with skill drills.

About the author . . .

If there is such a thing as a master teacher of young children, **Victoria Denny** surely qualifies. She has the unique long-time experience needed to successfully teach the little ones at the primary level.

Author: Victoria Denny
Editor: Lee Quackenbush
Artists: Jim Price/Carol Tiernon
Cover Art: Jan Vonk

128